THE BUSINESS OF
CRITICISM

Oxford University Press, Amen House, London E.C.4

GLASGOW NEW YORK TORONTO MELBOURNE WELLINGTON
BOMBAY CALCUTTA MADRAS KARACHI LAHORE DACCA
CAPE TOWN SALISBURY NAIROBI IBADAN ACCRA
KUALA LUMPUR HONG KONG

THE BUSINESS OF CRITICISM

BY

HELEN GARDNER

OXFORD
AT THE CLARENDON PRESS

FIRST EDITION 1959
REPRINTED 1959, 1960
REPRINTED LITHOGRAPHICALLY IN GREAT BRITAIN
AT THE UNIVERSITY PRESS, OXFORD
FROM SHEETS OF THE FIRST EDITION
1962

TO
DAVID AND JOANNA WILSON

PREFACE

THE two sets of lectures which are printed together here were each given in response to special invitations. The first series, 'The Profession of a Critic', was delivered in the University of London in the spring of 1953, in response to an invitation to give three lectures, on a subject of my own choice, to students engaged in research in English Literature. I had just published my edition of John Donne's *Divine Poems*, and had no 'work in progress' sufficiently advanced to be worthy of the occasion. I decided that I would take an opportunity to ask myself what, after twenty-five years of teaching and writing, I thought my aim was. The lectures have been expanded from lecture form and documented; but they are substantially unaltered.

The second series, 'The Limits of Literary Criticism', was given at King's College, Newcastle, in the spring of 1956, in response to an invitation from the University of Durham to deliver the Riddell Memorial Lectures for that year. They were published in the autumn of that year and are reprinted here without alteration. The terms of the Deed of Foundation for these lectures demand that the lectures should be concerned with the relation between religion and contemporary developments of thought, 'with particular emphasis on and reference to the bearing of such developments on the Ethics and Tenets of Christianity'. The audience for these lectures was not, therefore, an audience whose primary interest was in English Literature. This accounts for their emphasis. It made me discuss rather fully the work of an influential New

Testament critic, but not single out any particular critics of literature for discussion.

Although the two sets of lectures had different terms of reference, I hope I am right in thinking that they to some extent complement each other. Both argue the necessity of an historical approach to works of literature and the twin necessity of recognizing the historical nature of our own approach. Both are concerned with the nature of revelation, which if it is to take place at all, must do so in a certain place and at a certain time, but, if it is a true revelation, cannot be bounded by its circumstances. Both are pleas for a certain measure of scepticism, which, while we pursue with our utmost energy and intelligence different paths towards the 'meaning' of what we read, will preserve us from thinking that the meaning can be exhausted by our effort: 'Uno itinere non potest perveniri ad tam grande secretum.' For my title I have adapted some words from Dryden, who, although he deplorably referred to *Queen Gorboduc* and, worse still, declared it was in rhyme (which proves he had not read it), sums up for me the purpose which any research I may undertake subserves:

They wholly mistake the nature of criticism who think its business is principally to find fault. Criticism, as it was first instituted by Aristotle, was meant a standard of judging well; the chiefest part of which is, to observe those excellencies which should delight a reasonable reader.

It is to 'the common sense of readers uncorrupted with literary prejudices' that the critic must ultimately appeal. By this, 'after all the refinements of subtilty and the dogmatism of learning', his work, like the poet's, will finally be judged.

HELEN GARDNER

St. Hilda's College
Oxford

CONTENTS

The Profession of a Critic

The Limits of Literary Criticism
(Riddell Memorial Lectures, 1956)

The Profession of a Critic

I

THE SCEPTRE AND THE TORCH

By calling these lectures 'The Profession of a Critic' I suggest one thing, but I intend another. Criticism has increasingly in this century become professionalized, in the sense that one recognizes more and more, both here and in the United States, a tone in literary criticism which one can only call professional. It is the accent of someone who feels himself to speak with the authority which a certain discipline or training gives. There is very little feeling in critical writing today of someone loving to 'fold his legs and have out his talk'. A certain severity and strenuousness reigns. The notion that anybody with natural taste, some experience of life, a decent grounding in the classics, and the habit of wide reading can talk profitably on English Literature is highly unfashionable. The cynic might point to other more sinister signs of professionalism: the esoteric and almost unintelligible vocabulary of some critics; the appearance of a Dictionary of Critical Terms, comparable to a legal or medical dictionary; the embittered quarrels of rival sects, ranged under banners whose significance the lay mind can hardly appreciate; the fact that so many contributions to critical journals consist not of studies of a writer or his works, but of considerations of Mr. X's modifications of Mr. Y's criticism of Mr. Z's article on—shall we say *Measure for Measure*, or Marvell's 'The Garden'? The ordinary cultured reader, picking up such a journal, feels like someone entering a cinema in the middle of a gangster film, baffled about the antecedents of the battle which is raging, and uncertain who is fighting on whose side. He might well find himself less at sea if he picked up the *Lancet* or the *Law Quarterly Review*.

We may deplore some of these developments and mock at others; but it has to be recognized that some such developments are inevitable. The amateur is being squeezed out in every field by the immense extensions of knowledge and of the technical means for acquiring it. Problems which did not exist for Johnson confront the modern critic. They have been created by the growth of historical science, with the consequent development of the historical sense, by the growth of psychological science, which has profoundly modified our whole conception of the motivation of human activities, including speech, and by the growth of sociology, with its ally anthropology, which asks us to see a work of art not merely in relation to its author but as the expression of the culture in which it was created. Further, there is for the literary critic the task of coming to terms with the growth of linguistic studies: the development of the historical study of the English language on the one hand, and of the philosophic study of language on the other. The critic today reads an author of the sixteenth or seventeenth century haunted by a sense that although what he reads is apparently written in the language which he himself speaks, in various, subtle ways it is not; and merely looking up the hard words in the *Oxford English Dictionary* does not help, because it is in the ordinary words that the traps lie. He hardly dares to talk of the 'music of

Shakespeare's verse', because he is uncertain of the quality or the quantity of the vowels and of possible shifts in the accentuation of words. And if he decides to ignore the findings of the historians of the English language, and take it that Shakespeare 'means' what he means today and that his 'music' is whatever music a modern ear finds in his verse, he is disturbed by echoes of the dimly understood debates of modern logicians, who have undermined the simple assumption that we all know what something *means*, or indeed that we know what *meaning* itself is.

This widening of the intellectual horizon has gone on side by side with a multiplication of aids to knowledge which makes the task of being well informed on any topic extremely arduous. More and more libraries are catalogued, more and more records calendared; there are bibliographies of bibliographies and indexes of indexes. Most of all, the inventions of the photostat and the microfilm have made the contents of all the libraries of the world accessible. An editor today has no excuse, except the weakness of the flesh, for not examining all known manuscripts of a work. A critic can find it only too easy to defer making up his mind while he studies what is rather ironically called 'the literature of the subject'. He cannot plead justifiable ignorance of the researches or opinions of a Chinese or Peruvian professor. He should have known of them if he had kept abreast of the bibliographies and reports of 'work in progress'. Even unpublished theses, which used to lie unread in the stack-rooms of libraries, are now indexed and can be microfilmed.

Some degree of professionalism is, I imagine, unavoidable in all intellectual pursuits today. What seems uncertain is what is meant by 'the discipline of literary criticism'—a phrase that is often used; and what sort of training and what standards should be taken for granted by someone who regards himself as a literary critic. The title I have chosen suggests that I am going to attempt to answer these questions; but I am not. It is only too apparent that a great many critics today, who appear to have in common a sense of criticism as a profession, hold very different views on what equipment the critic needs and what his purpose or function is. I have taken refuge therefore in the indefinite article, and also in the ambiguity—blessed word—of the word 'profession'. I am not concerning myself with critics and criticism in general; but with what I, as an individual, feel to be involved in the act of literary criticism and with what I have come to feel to be its discipline. I am using the word 'profession' in its older sense, for in the sense in which law and medicine are professions, criticism can never be one. Criticism is an art, although only a minor one. It is impossible to conceive—or at least I hope it is—of a General Critical Council, holding diploma examinations, awarding a right to practise and stigmatizing certain practitioners for unprofessional conduct and striking them off its register. I am taking an opportunity to scrutinize and avow the beliefs which underlie my own practice as a critic. I am not prepared to define what qualifications are necessary before one can be regarded as professionally equipped to criticize, and I am not disturbed by the thought that many critics whose work I admire and read with profit and pleasure might, if pressed, give a very different account of their beliefs and practices.

The primary critical act is a judgement, the decision that a certain piece of writing has significance and value. It asserts a hold in some way upon my intellect, which entertains the propositions which it makes. It appeals through my senses and imagination to my capacity to recognize order and harmony and to be delighted by them. It appeals also to my experience as a human being, to my conscience and moral life. I put the triad in this order because in literature, whose medium is words, unintelligibility prevents recognition of the presence of either beauty or wisdom. We must feel that the work 'makes sense', even if at first only in patches, if we are to feel its value. But, of course, in experience we are not conscious of these different kinds of value as distinct. It is only for purposes of analysis, and when we come to try to rationalize our responses, that we separate what is in a work of art not separable: what it says, how it says it, and why what it says is important to us.

This response to a work as having value is the beginning of fruitful critical activity as I see it. The critic's function then is to assist his readers to find the value which he believes the work to have. To attempt to measure the amount of value, to declare or attempt to demonstrate that this poem is more valuable than that, or to range writers in an order of merit does not seem to me to be the true purpose of criticism. Such attempts ignore the nature of taste and the nature of values. Good taste is not an absolute. Two persons of excellent taste and judgement may differ strongly on the relative merits of two works; and the attempt to rank writers in a literary hierarchy ignores the obvious fact that certain writers and certain works mean more to some ages and to some persons than to others, and that our responses vary very greatly with our circumstances and our age. Statements about relative values are either unnecessary, elaborate attempts to prove what cannot be proved and can only be accepted as established by the judgement of the ages,[1] or else they are rationalizations of personal and temporary tastes and prejudices. *King Lear* needs no tributes now. We have no need to argue its claim to greatness: it has long ago passed the test of 'length of duration and continuance of esteem'. Equally, it would be a waste of time to demonstrate what nobody would deny, that it is a greater work than *Love's Labour's Lost*; or to debate whether it is or is not superior to *Hamlet*. I have no desire to find reasons for finding less or more enjoyment in Herbert's poetry than I do in Marvell's. I prefer to attempt to deepen my understanding and enjoyment of both and am grateful for diversity of gifts and the difference of one star from another in glory. When Wordsworth wrote

> If thou indeed derive thy light from Heaven
> Then, to the measure of that heaven-born light,
> Shine, Poet! in thy place, and be content:—

he was not inviting us to apportion their proper places to the poets, though he, of course, took for granted that some stars are larger and brighter than others, as also that their largeness

[1] 'To works, of which the excellence is not absolute and definite, but gradual and comparative; to works not raised upon principles demonstrative and scientifick, but appealing wholly to observation and experience, no other test can be applied than length of duration and continuance of esteem.' Having granted to Shakespeare 'the privilege of established fame and prescriptive veneration', Johnson went on to assert that it was 'proper to inquire by what peculiarities of excellence *Shakespeare* has gained and kept the favour of his countrymen' (*Preface to Shakespeare*). His criticism of Shakespeare, where he accepted posterity's verdict, is happier than his attempt to demonstrate that *Samson Agonistes* is a tragedy 'which ignorance has admired and bigotry applauded' and that 'no man could have fancied that he read *Lycidas* with pleasure, had he not known its author'.

and brightness may vary with times and seasons. Comparison is a most valuable tool by which to bring out the individuality of the writers compared. When used to attempt to set one up and put another down it usually reveals not objective standards of value by which writers may be ranked, but imperfect sympathies in the critic.

This is not, I hope I need hardly say, a plea for the indiscriminate acceptance of all writing which has had the good luck to survive the ravages of time. Nor do I mean that it is not part of the critic's function to distinguish failures in conception and execution. This is often an essential part of the disengaging of the essential value of a writer or his work. But anyone capable of intellectual growth can remember with amusement, and possibly some shame, youthful ineptitudes which seemed at the time to be 'discriminating evaluations'. We have often much less need to blush for earlier enthusiasms which have not stood the test of time. To have seen more promise of value than the work came in time to provide is less destructive to the development of right judgement and true taste than to have been superior to what is of value. Critics are wise to leave alone those works which they feel a crusading itch to attack and writers whose reputations they feel a call to deflate. Only too often it is not the writer who suffers ultimately but the critic:

> The man recover'd of the bite
> The dog it was that died.

When the dust and flurry of the argument has subsided, the writer has not been 'dislodg'd'. He is still there:

> Still green with bays each ancient Altar stands
> Above the reach of sacrilegious hands.

'The rudiment of criticism', wrote Mr. T. S. Eliot, 'is the ability to choose a good poem and reject a bad poem; and its most severe test is of its ability to select a good *new* poem, to respond properly to a new situation.'[1] This suggests that there is in all 'good poems' a kind of essence which the critic, like a sensitive dog, should with one sniff distinguish; and it suggests that poems can be absolutely divided into 'good poems' and 'bad poems', whereas from the universally acknowledged masterpiece to the total failure there is a whole range where praise or blame, interest or indifference, is quite properly qualified by the critic's personal predilections. To demand this unerring apportioning of a pass or fail mark is to confuse the critic with the connoisseur. The rudiment of criticism is not so much the power to distinguish any good poem from any bad poem, as the power to respond to a good poem and to be able to elucidate its significance, beauty, and meaning in terms which are valid for other readers. And by a 'good poem' I am content to mean a poem which is agreed to be so by lovers of poetry, or which the critic can convince such lovers is a good poem, by making them aware of the significance, beauty, and meaning which he finds in it. If the severest test of criticism is the ability to give good tips in the Parnassus stakes, to spot the winners, some of our greatest critics must be judged to have failed the test. But our judgement of Coleridge as probably our greatest literary critic is not qualified by his extravagant admiration when young for the sonnets of the Rev. William Bowles, or by his failure when old to be excited by the work of his younger contemporaries. Keats, reading the first two cantos of *Don Juan* on publication, saw in them

[1] *The Use of Poetry and the Use of Criticism*, 1933, p. 18.

only 'a paltry originality'. This signal failure to 'respond properly to a new situation' does not affect our admiration for him as a critic of extraordinary insight. Coleridge and Keats are great critics because of what they tell us of the nature of the poetic imagination and of the power of poetry, and because the things they have to say about certain poets, notably Shakespeare, permanently affect our own reading of those poets. The capacity to ponder works of art and to say something which enlarges our conception of their value, or gives them a fresh relevance, is the rudiment of criticism as an art. This explains why, on the whole, criticism which has survived its own day is rarely concerned with the critic's contemporaries, unless, as with Coleridge on Wordsworth, the critic has been deeply implicated with his subject. Coleridge writing on Wordsworth cannot be said to be 'responding to a new situation'. Mr. Eliot's own critical writings are a case in point. No poet, I suppose, in all history has been more aware of the contemporary situation or more generous in praise and encouragement of younger writers; but his own criticism has been almost wholly concerned with the literature of the past. A conviction of value needs the test of experience and time. Literary journalism and literary reporting are valuable and highly skilled activities, requiring great gifts and fulfilling an important literary function. But the capacity to write significant criticism is not the same as the power to make a rapid, immediate judgement. They may be linked, but frequently they are not. And the power to see deeply, which the critic needs, may be linked, though it need not be, with an inability to see widely.

In Johnson's allegory in the third number of *The Rambler*

Criticism is the eldest daughter of Labour and Truth, committed at birth to the care of Justice and brought up in the palace of Wisdom. She was 'appointed the governess of Fancy, and impowered to beat time to the chorus of the Muses, when they sung before the throne of Jupiter'. When the Muses descended to the lower world she accompanied them. Justice bestowed a sceptre upon her, to be held in her right hand. With this she could confer immortality or oblivion. 'In her left hand, she bore an unextinguishable torch, manufactured by Labour and lighted by Truth, of which it was the particular quality immediately to show everything in its true form, however it might be disguised to common eyes.' But she found herself confronted with so many works in which beauties and faults were equally mingled that, 'for fear of using improperly the sceptre of Justice', she 'referred the cause to be considered by Time', whose proceedings, 'though very dilatory, were, some few caprices excepted, conformable to justice'. Before returning to heaven she broke her sceptre, one end of which was seized by Flattery, and the other by Malevolence.

Johnson's onslaught on the critics of his own day provides me with a convenient metaphor. I do not feel any call to wield the sceptre. This is not solely because with the poetry of the past the fact that it speaks at all over the years is evidence that it has some value, and the question of how much or how little does not seem to me a profitable subject to discuss; and with the poetry of the present all verdicts must be proved right or wrong by time. My fundamental reason for rejecting the notion that the fundamental task of the critic is the erection and application of standards by which writers and their works

are to be given their ratings is that the enterprise seems to
me not merely futile but deleterious. If a critic is to be judged
by his success in giving just the right amount of approval,
then he, and the common reader who is to learn from him, is
required to take up an attitude to works of art which is highly
inimical to their proper enjoyment, whether they are works
which give profound delight, or works which give lesser
pleasures. A mind which is concerned with being right, which
is nervously anxious not to be taken in, which sits in judgement, and approaches works of passion and imagination with
neatly formulated demands, is inhibited from the receptiveness
and disinterestedness which are the conditions of aesthetic
experience. The attempt to train young people in this kind of
discrimination seems to me to be a folly, if not a crime. The
young need, on the one hand, to be encouraged to read for
themselves, widely, voraciously, and indiscriminately; and,
on the other, to be helped to read with more enjoyment and
understanding what their teachers have found to be of value.
Exuberance and enthusiasm are proper to the young, as
Quintilian remarked: 'The young should be daring and in-
ventive and should rejoice in their inventions, even though
correctness and severity are still to be acquired.' And he
added that to his mind 'the boy who gives least promise is
one in whom judgement develops in advance of the imagination'.[1] True personal discrimination or taste develops slowly
and probably best unconsciously. It cannot be forced by exer-
cises in selecting the good and rejecting the bad by the application of stock critical formulas: it may indeed be stunted.[2] It

[1] *Institutio Oratoria*, II. iv. 6–7.
[2] Proust's comment on the attempt to impose adult tastes on children is

comes, if it is to come at all, by growth in understanding and enjoyment of the good. 'Principium veritatis res admirari.' Knowledge begins in wonder and wonder will find and develop its own proper discipline. True judgement or wisdom in a critic can only come in the same way as all wisdom does: 'For the very true beginning of her is the desire of discipline and the care of discipline is love.'

The torch rather than the sceptre would be my symbol for the critic. Elucidation, or illumination, is the critic's primary task as I conceive it. Having made the initial act of choice, or judgement of value, I want to remove any obstacles which prevent the work having its fullest possible effect. Because a poem already speaks to me, I want to find ways to ensure that, as far as possible, it says to me what it has to say and not what I want it to say, and that it says it in its own way and not in mine. I say 'as far as possible', because of 'Nature's Law'

> By which all Causes else according still
> To the reception of thir matter act,
> Not to th'extent of thir own Spheare.

Comprehension is limited by the capacity of the comprehender, and inexhaustibility is one of the marks of a work of art. But although we have only our own eyes to see through, we can train them to see better, and we can make use of

valid for all attempts to force aesthetic consciences. His hero is remembering pictures which he loved as a child, 'œuvres naïvement incomplètes comme étaient mes propres impressions et que les sœurs de ma grand'mère s'indignaient de me voir aimer. Elles pensaient qu'on doit mettre devant les enfants, et qu'ils font preuve de goût en aimant d'abord, les œuvres que, parvenu à la maturité, on admire définitivement. C'est sans doute qu'elles se figuraient les mérites esthétiques comme des objets matériels qu'un œil ouvert ne peut faire autrement que de percevoir, sans avoir eu besoin d'en mûrir lentement des équivalents dans son propre cœur.'

instruments, such as spectacles, telescopes, or microscopes, to supplement our natural powers of vision.

The beginning of the discipline of literary criticism lies in the recognition of the work of art's objective existence as the product of another mind, which exists not to be used but to be understood and enjoyed. Its process is the progressive correction of misconceptions, due to ignorance, personal prejudice, or temperamental defects, the setting of the work at a distance, the disentangling it from my personal hopes, fears, and beliefs, so that the poem which my mind re-creates in the reading becomes more and more a poem which my own mind would never have created. If the first response to a work of art is wonder, the child of wonder is curiosity. The satisfaction of curiosity, which is a great pleasure, brings a renewal of the sense of wonder and so leads to further curiosity. The last word is never said.

> To know, can only wonder breede,
> And not to know, is wonders seede.

The enlarging and continual reforming of one's conception of a work by bringing fresh knowledge and fresh experience of life and literature to it, this process of continual submission and resubmission to the work, is highly delightful and perpetually renews the original sense of delight from which the critic began. Wordsworth, who we know found composition laborious and exhausting, insisted again and again on the 'overbalance of enjoyment' which accompanied the poet's sympathies, however painful the objects which called them out. He declared that the poet prompted by this feeling of pleasure, is accompanied by pleasure throughout his studies. To this 'grand elementary feeling of pleasure' Wordsworth referred all intellectual activity, seeing it as the motive force of the man of science—the chemist, mathematician, and anatomist—as much as of the poet. But beyond the pleasure that there is in all intellectual activity, the delight in the satisfaction of curiosity, in the serious inquisition of truth, and in the ordering of our experience into rationally intelligible statements, the critic of literature, like all students of the fine arts, has a special kind of pleasure in his work. He is continually in the company of his intellectual and spiritual betters. He is concerned with things which are precious to his readers as well as to himself. His task is 'to add sunshine to daylight, by making the happy happier': to help himself and his readers to understand more deeply and to enjoy more fully what he and they already understand and enjoy. I feel little confidence in the judgements of any critic who does not make me feel, however minute his analysis, and however laborious his researches may have·been, that his motive force has been enjoyment. We do not need to disguise our good fortune, as if to allow the world to see that the study of literature is enjoyable might diminish its intellectual respectability.[1]

When I say that the beginning of the discipline of literary criticism lies in the recognition of the objective existence of a work of art, I am not denying the truth in Mr. Eliot's saying that the meaning of a poem is 'what the poem means to different sensitive readers'.[2] This is not, in its context, and in the

---

[1] 'Gloom and solemnity are entirely out of place in even the most rigorous study of an art originally intended to make glad the heart of man. "Gravity, a mysterious carriage of the body to conceal the defects of the mind" (Laurence Sterne).' Ezra Pound, *ABC of Reading*, 1934, p. xi.

[2] 'The Frontiers of Criticism' in *On Poetry and Poets*, 1957, p. 113.

general context of Mr. Eliot's criticism, a justification of sub-jective criticism, but a plea for what Lascelles Abercrombie pleaded for in a famous lecture, 'liberty of interpretation'. He was concerned with one form of critical tyranny: the refusal to allow a work to gather meaning through the ages. Mr. Eliot is protesting, also I think rightly, at another: the tendency of some modern interpretative criticism to trespass into an area where the reader has the right to demand to be left alone with the poem. This is the area of aesthetic experience, which must, of its nature, be personal, conditioned by the individual's ex-perience of life and art. The critic's task is to assist his readers to read for themselves, not to read for them. He must respect their sensibilities by not obtruding his own. He is not writing to display his own ingenuity, subtlety, learning, or sensitive-ness; but to display the work in a manner which will enable it to exert its own power.

All works of art, whatever else they may be, are historical objects, and to approach them as such is, I believe, a funda-mental necessity if they are to realize their power fully over us. 'All good art is contemporary' is a well-known critical maxim. It needs to be balanced by the statement that 'All art, including contemporary art, is historical.' One of the main difficulties in coming to terms with contemporary art is the difficulty we have in thinking of ourselves and our own age as historical. We know both too much and too little of our own context to see the work in perspective. Certain elements in it have an adventitious value; others we are unable to see. Every work of art is the product of a point in space and time, in so far as it would certainly have been different if it had appeared in any other place and time. It could not have been what it is but for the art which went before it. We ourselves see it through our knowledge and experience of what has come after it. It is historical also as the product of a mind which grew through particular experiences and not through others; and each particular work has an historical relation to its author's other works.

Attempts have been made in this century to ignore these truisms, or to depreciate their importance. The work of art has been treated as autonomous and self-explanatory, and the pure critic has tried to concern himself with the poem as it can be explained purely in terms of itself and himself. Loosed from its moorings in place and time, the poem is conceived as floating like a balloon, with the critic caught up to meet it in the clouds. This attempt to isolate the work of art and treat it as a thing *per se*, putting it under a kind of mental bell-jar, disregards the nature of art, and makes criticism a special kind of activity, divorced from our normal habits as readers. The ideal which is aimed at approximates to the scientist in his laboratory, as opposed to the student in his library, the chemist faced with a substance to analyse, rather than the reader bringing his human experience to the book he is reading, who is listening to 'a man speaking to men'. The critics who tried to perform these feats of levitation, or to achieve this rigorous exclusiveness, were, in fact, usually highly sophisticated and well-educated persons who were only playing at being ignorant of historical and biographical facts. Those who claimed that they were interpreting a poem of Donne's 'by itself' actually knew a good deal about Donne and the history and literature of his age, although they might have done better if they had tried to learn a little more. They were not really reacting to the poem as they would have to a poem by an unknown contemporary, met with accidentally in a newspaper. Luckily Dr. I. A. Richards undertook the experiment of presenting poems 'by themselves', without even an author's name attached, to classes of undergraduates, and published the results in the protocols in *Practical Criticism*. The experiment proved, I think, not the incapacity of the readers, but the futility of the method. Quite apart from the inhibiting anxiety of many of the readers to say the right thing or not to be taken in, it was clear that, divorced from their human and historical context, works were deprived of their power to speak to the heart and conscience. The young person who was faced with Donne's sonnet on the Last Judgement,

> At the round earth's imagined corners blow
> Your trumpets, angels . . .

and commented that the poem expressed 'the simple faith of a very simple man' was not making at all an idiotic comment. There is nothing in the language of this poem to suggest to a reader looking at it on a sheet of paper in a classroom that it was written over three hundred years ago, and no educated Christian today would write in these literal terms of the general Resurrection at the Last Day. It was to the reader's credit that he at least recognized that the poem was written out of such a literal faith. If a poem such as this is to communicate its intense religious feeling, we must accept the terms in which it speaks to us, which are the terms of its age. The necessity of an historical sense if the works of the past are to have a present value to us and not appear quaint or, as in this case, intellectually absurd, is seen in the difficulty each generation has in reading the works of its immediate predecessors. There is nearly always a kind of dead period when works of art sink in repute and interest because they are near enough to seem old-fashioned but not far enough off to have become historical. They have lost the power to 'speak to our condition'; but as soon as they can be felt to be historical they regain a contemporary relevance.

How to make a proper use of historical and biographical information and of the facts of literary history is a fundamental problem for the critic. The deepening of historical apprehension in his readers, the provision of a context for the work, is one of the main ways in which he can assist them in their approach to the meaning of the work. I say 'approach to the meaning' because of the paradox that the more we put a poem into the past, establish it in its historical context, and interpret it by its own age's aesthetic canons, the more its uniqueness and individuality appear. When we are unfamiliar with the art of an epoch all its products tend to seem alike. The better we come to know a period, the less its products appear 'period pieces'. The historical approach takes us towards the meaning and can explain much; but the value of a poem does not lie in its power to tell us how men once thought and felt. It has an extra-historical life, which makes what had significance, beauty, and meaning in its own age have significance, beauty, and meaning now. The total meaning of a work of art cannot be analysed or treated historically, though I believe we cannot approach it except through history as we ourselves meet it in history. It is extra-historical, I believe, because it is the expression and creation of a human mind and personality and so is ultimately irreducible into anything but itself. The mystery of the survival of the significance of works of art brings one face to face with the mystery of human personality. A critic's attitude to works of art must depend ultimately on his conception of the nature of man. Those who hold seriously to enjoyment as the true end of reading speak from within the Greek tradition which rates the life of contemplation above the life of action and holds that man's destiny is to enjoy the vision of truth, beauty, and goodness, or, to use the Christian formulation, 'to glorify God and to enjoy him for ever'. And the critic who, in addition, believes that the true meaning of a work of art can only be apprehended by seeing it within its historical context, but that its meaning is not limited by that context, is one who has to some degree or other parted company with Plato and does not believe that man is a soul imprisoned in a body, but that the union of soul and body makes man.

'Books are not absolutely dead things', wrote Milton. 'A good book is the precious life-blood of a master-spirit, embalmed and treasured up on purpose to a life beyond life.' This is nearer my way of thinking about a poem, or a play, or a novel, than the conception of a work as 'a well-wrought urn', even though it is an urn containing the 'greatest ashes'. As a counterpoise to the sense of the work as historically conditioned, the critic needs a sense of the work's quiddity or essence, its individuality, as a particular expression of a personal response to experience, a personal vision of the world. This sense of the work's individuality can be deepened by the reading of the author's other works and can be aided by the knowledge gained by various means of the author's life. Insistence on the impersonality of the poet or the poem seems to me to be a heresy which has arisen, as most heresies have, from a reaction against imperfect and vulgarized notions of the truth. To treat a poem purely as an artifact and analyse it solely in terms of its rhetorical structure, is to ignore, in an attempt to make criticism pure, the facts of our experience as readers. In our reading we recognize individual voices and respond to individual visions. We find in an author's various works the impress of an individual mind whose quality we come to know. The desire to know all we can about this mind—to know Shakespeare, as well as to know *Hamlet*, *King Lear*, or *The Tempest*—is the natural result of contact with it in one work, and indeed an obvious way to understand that work better. The writer's personal history, like the pressure of the age in which he lived, is a context which can help us to focus on the work as it is. Although much biographical information may be irrelevant, the critic cannot afford to be ignorant of facts which may assist him to learn the habit of an author's mind, or the circumstances in which a work was written, which may, in that particular work, have affected that habit. Biographical knowledge can sharpen the sense of the work's objective existence, as itself, distinct and meaningful in itself. This sense of the work's originality can be stimulated and enriched also by the study of an author's sources, not merely his direct sources, but also his indirect, that is, his general reading. I suppose one of the best examples of such enrichment is the effect that reading Livingstone Lowes's *The Road to Xanadu* has on our response to *The Ancient Mariner*. This pioneer study not only illustrated the workings of the poetic faculty; it gave a new dimension to the poem. Although it was itself an investigation of the poem's origins, rather than a study of the poem, it called our attention, as no previous criticism had, to certain elements in the structure, narrative details, and diction of the poem, and added to the overtones of the narrative echoes of greatly told stories of adventure and endurance.

I have continually recurred in this discussion to the words 'the work itself'. Although I have a quarrel over method with the 'new critics', for their rejection of the historical aspect of a work of art, fundamentally I am on their side. The ultimate end of scholarship and literary history and biographical study for me is the assistance it will give to the elucidation of a work of art. Of course these activities have their own value and interest; but as far as I am concerned they serve a greater end. My primary concern is with the work itself, not as part of an author's total *œuvre*, certainly not as a psychological or sociological document, or as a piece of historical evidence, and not as a link in the chain of a literary tradition. I want to study it for what it has to give which extends and strengthens my imaginative apprehension and understanding of life. When Mr. Eliot says 'I am more and more interested, not in one play or another, but in Shakespeare's work as a whole', I should tend to disagree and say that fundamentally I feel a desire to elucidate certain works which have come to have great value for me. But since knowledge of all the writer's works is desirable for the fullest understanding of each, and knowledge of each is required for the understanding of his work as a whole, the point is a fine one. To concentrate upon the single work, the created whole, is the thing which I feel most called upon to do. The discovery of a work's centre, the source of its life in all its parts, and response to its total movement—a word I prefer to 'structure', for time is inseparable from our apprehension of works of literature—is to me the purpose of critical activity. And if I ask myself why I write criticism I think the answer is that since it is true

> That no man is the lord of anything—
> Though in and of him there be much consisting—
> Till he communicate his parts to others:

I write because the attempt to formulate satisfactory answers to questions which arise from the work itself makes the work more meaningful to me. It is, in the end, for my own sake and not for any other purpose, that I hold up the torch, manufactured by labour, and lighted, I hope, by truth.

II

THE HISTORICAL APPROACH

In an essay on 'The Sense of the Past',[1] Professor Lionel Trilling observes: 'To suppose that we can think like men of another time is as much of an illusion as to suppose that we can think in a wholly different way'; and he adds: 'It ought to be for us a real question whether, and in what way, human nature is always the same.' The justice of the observation and the pertinence of the question are shown by the fact that we can hardly conceive of such a statement being made, or of such a question being posed, before about the middle of the last century.

Dryden, in this as in other things, deserves the title of being the first modern critic. He is aware, as his predecessors are not, that poets are 'of an age'. He means more by this than Ben Jonson did when he said Shakespeare was not 'of an age', but 'for all time'. To Dryden every poet is to some degree 'of an age' and one of his fundamental critical positions is that 'the genius of every age is different'.[2] Along with many of his contemporaries he had an acute sense of the time he lived in as 'an age', and he is constantly concerned with the relation of his own poetry and plays to contemporary tastes and fashions.

[1] Reprinted in *The Liberal Imagination,* 1950.
[2] *An Essay of Dramatic Poesy,* 1668. The earliest use of the term 'the Genius of the age' recorded in *O.E.D.* is 1665.

His sense of period, which he extended from his own sense that the Elizabethans were writers of 'the last age', is one of his most valued weapons as a critic. He uses it to reconcile his acceptance of the standards of his own day with his admiration of the poetry of the past. What would be gross in a modern writer can be excused in an Elizabethan, since the manners and tastes of his age were different. It is also a means by which he can indulge in his favourite exercise of comparison and bring together writers who, at first sight, seem too far apart to be compared. If we make proper allowances for the differences between the age of Augustus and the later empire, Horace and Juvenal can be set side by side as satirists. As always, Dryden is content to open up a way of thinking without feeling any need to explore its implications and make clear his theoretical position. But his implications are quite clear. In spite of his constant references to 'the age' of writers, he assumes, though he never actually states the position, that if you will allow for the differences between one period and another, you will find them comparatively unimportant. Poets of all ages and all tongues can be compared on a basis of what is common to them: the 'general nature' which they imitate, the life and passions of men. He takes the same attitude here as he does to the parallel problem of differences of language, where he is also a critical pioneer. Just as 'a thing well said will be wit in all languages', so a passion well painted will be true in all periods and for all time. Dryden deals lightly with the historical because he is writing before the development of the historical imagination. He has historical information to hand, and thinks it should be used: he does not think historically.

Johnson also took the historical in his stride. He had far

more historical knowledge than Dryden, and, with his work as lexicographer and editor behind him, is the patron of all scholar-critics, as Dryden is the patron of all men of letters and of the poet turned critic. But their fundamental position is the same.

In order to make a true estimate of the abilities and merit of a writer, it is always necessary to examine the genius of his age, and the opinions of his contemporaries. A poet who should now make the whole action of his tragedy depend upon enchantment, and produce the chief events by the assistance of supernatural agents, would be censured as transgressing the bounds of probability, be banished from the Theatre to the nursery, and condemned to write fairy tales instead of tragedies.

So Johnson opens his long and very learned note on the first stage-direction of *Macbeth*: 'Enter three Witches.' And he concludes:

Upon this general infatuation *Shakespeare* might be easily allowed to found a play, especially since he has followed with great exactness such histories as were then thought true; nor can it be doubted that the scenes of enchantment, however they may now be ridiculed, were both by himself and his audience thought awful and affecting.

Johnson suggests here, *en passant*, that we ought to take into our account how a work appeared to its first audiences, a theory much in vogue today. He does not appeal to the audience to help him to interpret the work, a dangerous enterprise which often involves the critic who attempts it in a perfectly circular argument. He appeals to the audience to acquit Shakespeare from the charge of having chosen a childish plot. Johnson is dealing with something much more interesting and more difficult to handle than the changing manners and tastes and ideals of linguistic correctness which Dryden was concerned with. He is facing the problem of changing beliefs. How are we to respond to a work of art which embodies assumptions which were once accepted as true but are now unacceptable and appear to us as aberrations of the human intellect? He handles the problem with characteristic robustness, because, like Dryden, he is able to make a clear division. The historical is something to be got out of the way. The notion that we should ourselves find the scenes of enchantment 'awful and affecting' he does not consider for a moment. Changing beliefs, like changing customs and manners, are accidents. The whole basis of Johnson's criticism is the belief that human nature is always essentially the same and that the poet's concern is with general truth. He recognizes the genius of an age in order to discount it. Mrs. Thrale reports that he had not much respect for the study of History: 'He disliked the subject exceedingly and often said it took up room in a man's head which might be better filled.' To Johnson history means information about the past which makes it possible for the critic to find universal moral truth in ancient works of art. He praises Shakespeare for making 'nature predominate over accident': 'His story requires Romans and Kings, but he thinks only on men. . . . A poet overlooks the casual distinctions of country and condition.' Holding such views he can take up a commonplace like 'the Genius of an Age' without examining it or inquiring into it. His defective theory of the imagination, which he saw not as creative and magisterial but as ancillary to reason, allowed him to distinguish in a work such as *Macbeth* the 'Elizabethan' from that which is 'for all time'. What matters to him is that 'the danger of ambition is well described' and that 'the passions are directed to their true end'. The parts which now seem improbable may have had a moral intention once also: 'It was perhaps necessary to warn credulity against vain and illusive predictions.'

Criticism after Coleridge, which accepts as axiomatic the integrity of a work of art as the product of a creative imagination, cannot make this distinction between the kernel of eternal moral truth and the shell of outmoded belief. Coleridge himself, although eager enough to use an historical argument in defence of romantic drama against neo-classical, when he approaches the work itself salves its imaginative integrity by ignoring the historical. 'The weird sisters are as true a *creation* of Shakespeare's as are his Ariel and Caliban, the Fates, Furies and *materializing* witches being the elements.' This invites the question of what are the elements equivalent to 'the materializing witches' in the creation of Ariel and Caliban, and ignores the difference which Johnson sees clearly between comedy, where the fantasies of fairy-tale are in place, and tragedy, where they infect our sense of the seriousness of the issues with which the play is concerned. Coleridge's intense reverence for Shakespeare, and the strength with which he grasped the conception of the imagination as the prime and master faculty of the human mind, finding in it the image of the Creator, made him unwilling to take account of the limitations of the poet's historical situation. The greatest example of a fundamentally unhistoric approach is Coleridge's treatment of *Hamlet*. Like Johnson, it is the eternal which he looks for. But for that general knowledge of human life which

Johnson sought in poetry Coleridge substitutes knowledge of the working of the mind. 'Know mankind' becomes 'Know thyself'. 'He thought it essential to the understanding of *Hamlet* that we should reflect on the constitution of our own minds.' Coleridge no more questions than Johnson that human nature is always the same. But while Johnson makes allowance for the accidents of history, Coleridge ignores them. He thereby preserves the integrity of the work, but he does so at the cost of remaking it in his own image. He ignores the fact that *Hamlet* was written for the stage, and for a stage whose conventions were very different from the conventions of the stage of antiquity and the stage in his own day. He ignores also the fact that Shakespeare did not invent the story of *Hamlet*. Nobody would guess from reading Coleridge on *Hamlet* that the play had any other source than Shakespeare's imagination creating an image of human life as he knew it.

The great tradition which Coleridge inaugurated is still very powerful. Bradley's *Shakespearean Tragedy* stands in a direct line from him; and a study such as D. G. James's brief, but suggestive, *The Dream of Learning* (1951) shows the continuing strength, as well as the defects, of the unhistorical approach. The most interesting development from Coleridge is the attempt to interpret a work through the pattern of its images. This corresponds to developments in psychology since Coleridge's day and reflects the new knowledge of the workings of the mind gained by depth psychology. Its most notable exponent, Professor G. Wilson Knight, shows clearly his attitude to the temporal by calling his method 'spatial analysis'. It leads, I think, to a subjectivism far more extreme than Coleridge's. And in spite of Coleridge, Johnson's attitude still persists. It is well expressed by a great scholar-critic, Sir Herbert Grierson, like Johnson an editor:

For the lover of literature, literary history has an indirect value. He studies history that he may discount it. What he relishes in a poet of the past is exactly the same essential qualities as he enjoys in a poet of his own day—life and passion and art. But between us and every poet or thinker of the past hangs a thinner or thicker veil of outworn fashions and conventions. The same life has clothed itself in different garbs; the same passions have spoken in different images; the same art has adapted itself to different circumstances. To the historian these old clothes are in themselves a subject of interest. ... To the lover of literature they are, until by understanding he can discount them, a disadvantage because they invest the work of the poet with an irrelevant air of strangeness. He studies them that he may grow familiar with them and forget them, that he may clear and intensify his sense of what alone has permanent value, the poet's individuality and the art in which it is expressed.[1]

On the other side stand many scholars and historians and critics who agree with the sociologists and anthropologists— not to mention the dialectical materialists—and declare that all works of art are historically conditioned and that if you are to understand a poet you must understand him as the product of his age. In order to grasp what he is saying you must by an effort of the historical imagination leave in abeyance the assumptions of your own age and education, and attempt to make alive in your own mind the assumptions of his. You must consider the audience for whom he was writing, not merely to assess his success and failure in terms of the artistic standards of his day, but also to respond to him as they did. For, and it is here that Professor Trilling's questions arise,

[1] 'The Poetry of Donne', H. J. C. Grierson, *The Poems of John Donne*, 1912, vol. ii, p. vi.

you must, if you wish to understand a poet, live imaginatively in his period, re-create his intellectual environment, so that the whole complex situation in which he was born, grew up, and wrote is imaginatively familiar to you. Here, it is claimed, we can find objective standards of interpretation. If we want to understand Shakespeare we must read him 'as an Elizabethan would'. The assumption of the extreme historical school appears to be that the age is something which we can reach certainty about, and that armed with this certainty we can approach the unknown quantity, the play or poem.

The difficulty of attempting to turn oneself into an Elizabethan reader or spectator can easily be exposed. Historical investigation, which attempts to construct a narrative of what happened, can trace the development of the mining industry, or of astronomical thought, or of a literary style. Here we can clearly see achievement, the correction of error and the discovery of information. But the historical imagination which attempts to re-create a whole past situation is a very different matter. The historical imagination, itself of comparatively recent growth, is itself historically conditioned. Its weakness and contingency are obvious if we consider historical novels. Most of them are not even convincing at the time they are written, and as they recede into the past even those which seemed most successful are seen to tell us less and less about the age they were created to re-create and more and more about the age in which they were created. Contemporaries of Shorthouse found *John Inglesant* a wonderfully vivid and convincing re-creation of the climate of opinion in mid-seventeenth-century England. Anyone who reads it today reads it as a highly coloured romance which has the added interest of revealing very clearly the climate of opinion among English Churchmen after Newman's secession to Rome. Scrupulousness in avoiding anachronism in ideas and language makes no difference. The underlying assumptions of *Esmond* are unmistakably Victorian and Miss Rose Macaulay's *They Were Defeated*, although it uses no word which was not current in the seventeenth century, reflects clearly the mood of an intelligent and sensitive Liberal faced with the barbarity of the ideological conflicts of 'the thirties'. And if we turn from those rash enough to attempt to re-create the past in fiction to those who are content to describe it, the historians of various epochs, we find their emphasis shifts from decade to decade, so that 'the age' undergoes extraordinary transformations. In the last hundred years the conception of 'the Elizabethans' has been as unstable as the conception of *Hamlet*. To Froude and Kingsley they were God-fearing, Protestant, and patriotic. In the nineties they were Italianate and much less manly and God-fearing. In the twenties they were subtle, sensual, and sceptical. Recently they have become pious again, but in a different way, obsessed with the idea of hierarchy, the Great Chain of Being and Natural Law, crypto-Catholics and heirs to the Middle Ages. If I read the signs of the times rightly, they are now becoming rather more vigorous, adventurous, and Protestant again.[1]

I do not wish to suggest that one cannot and should not—

[1] I have in mind, of course, 'the Elizabethans' as they appear in literary history rather than as they appear in the works of historians proper. Literary students today seem as remote in their interests from historians as historians are from students of literature. It is as rare to find a student of literature who is acquainted with the work of Sir John Neale as to find an historian interested in recent work on Shakespeare or Spenser. Dr. A. L. Rowse is an honourable example of the second rarity.

indeed I hold that one must—build up over the years a conception of a writer's life and times which has some consistency
and which, though constantly modified, has yet some validity.
But the literary critic needs to be aware how provisional such
a conception is. It is an imaginative construction, made up of
scraps of information and insecure generalizations, influenced
by its creator's pre-conceptions, particular interests, and
historical circumstances. It needs to be kept fluid and not
allowed to harden into a fixed background. The fundamental
danger of the approach to a writer through the study of his
age is that it encourages us to attempt to interpret the concrete
by the abstract, the particular by the general, even more the
exceptional by the average. We are rightly sceptical when we
read statements about modern man and the modern mind and
dismiss both as figments of journalism. We ought to be at
least as sceptical about statements about the 'Elizabethan mind'.
The 'Elizabethan World Picture' tidily presented to us as a
system of thought cannot tell us how much of that picture had
truth and meaning for any single Elizabethan. And even if we
could discover a kind of highest common factor of contemporary beliefs and attitudes, it could not tell us what any individual
believed, and certainly not what Shakespeare believed. We do
not know very much about Shakespeare outside his plays, but
at least we know from them that he was not an average Elizabethan. Our sense of a period is far too arbitrary, unstable, and
conjectural to provide us with an objective field of reference by
which we can assert, 'This is what the work must have meant.'

The historical approach to a work of art is, as I see it, more
modest and tentative. Professor Trilling's suggestion, that to
suppose we can think like men of another time is an illusion,

seems to assume that we can think like men of our own time, or indeed like anyone else. We can understand, to a greater or less degree, how men of our day think if they try to communicate their thoughts to us. I have no idea how my silent companions in a bus or tube are thinking, although they, like me, have modern minds. If one speaks to me I can understand his thought; or, if I do not, I can ask him questions. I may have failed to grasp what he is saying because he has assumed that I have some information which in fact I do not possess. He has perhaps listened to the six o'clock news, or seen something in the stop press of his evening newspaper. Or perhaps he is speaking from assumptions which I do not share. When I ask him what he means he may tell me that he is a British Israelite, and then, if I want to understand what he has to say, I must listen while he explains his tenets to me. Or perhaps his mind is obsessed by some personal or family trouble, or is coloured by the circumstances in which he has grown up, and then I must listen while he explains to me what complex of feelings and events prompted a remark which it seemed to him important to make, but whose import I did not grasp. When we are confronted with the expression of the mind of someone long dead, embodied in a work of art, the process of coming to understand it seems to me fundamentally the same, although we cannot ask our questions directly. We have to develop a technique of questioning, asking questions which arise out of the work itself. We can only judge whether the answer to any particular question is a good answer by its consistency with our answers to other questions.

To illustrate what I mean I am going to consider some questions about *Hamlet*. An example of an unfruitful question, because it is too large and too general and leads inevitably to an answer which we ought to have known before we asked it, is the question which some writers seem to feel bound to raise before they approach a play built on the theme of revenge. What did the Elizabethans think of the ethics of private revenge? I have read more than one book in which the author establishes by detailed, indeed relentless, accumulation of statements by preachers and moralists that the Elizabethans thought murder unethical and private revenge sinful. What else should we expect preachers and moralists to say? Questions which lead us to platitudes and foregone conclusions are not worth asking. We might more profitably ponder over the temper of mind which lay behind the Bond of Association of 1584. The councillors who drafted this document, among them the pious Burghley, and the thousands up and down the country who signed it, pledged themselves 'in the presence of the eternal and ever-living God', whom they knew to have claimed vengeance as his prerogative, that, in the event of an attack on Elizabeth's person, they would 'prosecute to the death' any pretended successor to her throne by whom, or for whom, such an act should be attempted or committed. They swore 'to take the uttermost revenge on them . . . by any possible means . . . for their utter overthrow and extirpation'. That is, if Elizabeth were assassinated, Mary Stuart should be murdered, whether she were a party to the murder of her cousin or not, and beyond Mary, her son James, as a beneficiary of the crime. 'Discarding all scruples', comments Sir John Neale, 'they descended to the utter ruthlessness of their enemies.' These were law-abiding and God-fearing men. But they believed that the safety of the country and the preservation of the Protestant religion hung on the single life of Elizabeth. They were probably right in believing this. Perhaps if Elizabeth had met the same fate as William the Silent and Henry of Navarre, and England had fallen into the chaos of civil and religious wars, the play of *Hamlet*, along with other precious things, would not exist for us to talk about. We may be horrified at their forgetting that vengeance was forbidden by their religion, but we must recognize the appalling nature of their dilemma.

As an example of a fruitful question which it did not occur to Bradley to ask I would cite Professor Dover Wilson's question: 'What opinions were current when Shakespeare was writing about the nature of apparitions?' This is a modest question to which an answer can be found, and the answer Professor Dover Wilson found—that there was a conflict of opinion—is an illuminating one. It is consonant with the impression which the whole play makes upon us and adds to our feeling that Hamlet is moving in a world where there are no certainties. It casts light on the relation of Hamlet to Horatio. It gives meaning to a scene which had puzzled all critics, the cellarage scene. And, lastly, it casts a light upon the whole development of the play's action. By showing us how serious and widespread was the debate on the nature of ghosts, it makes us less ready to accept the notion that Hamlet arranges the play scene as an excuse for delaying his revenge. The information which Professor Dover Wilson made available to us strengthens our conception of Hamlet as a man of intellectual integrity and moral sensibility. To give a parallel from our own day: two hundred years hence, when, for all I know, modern psychology will seem as outmoded as alchemy or the theory of the humours, a critic, living in an age of chemical therapy, might fruitfully inquire what were some of the current opinions on the psychiatrist's role in society which might help to explain the rather ambiguous treatment of Reilly in Mr. Eliot's comedy *The Cocktail Party*. Mr. Eliot, as we are all perfectly aware without considering the matter at all, has been able to exploit for comic purposes our ambivalent feelings about 'mind doctors', as Shakespeare exploited for tragic purposes the conflict of opinion in his day about the reality and reliability of apparitions of departed persons. We are not asking what Mr. Eliot's own opinions about psychiatrists are, any more than we are asking whether Shakespeare believed in ghosts. Nor are we asking what attitude the plays demand that we should assume to the interference of Reilly or to the moral authority of the Ghost of Hamlet's father. These are questions which cannot be answered by historical inquiries alone, but historical inquiries can help us to answer them.

A much more complex and delicate question, which takes us near to the heart of the play, is raised by the complaint which Johnson makes about the plot of *Hamlet*. 'Hamlet is, through the whole play, rather an instrument than an agent. After he has, by the stratagem of the play, convicted the King, he makes no attempt to punish him, and his death is at last effected by an incident which Hamlet has no part in producing.' Bradley's celebrated question, which he thinks anyone would ask on hearing the plot of *Hamlet*, converts Johnson's objection to the conduct of the plot into censure of the conduct of the hero: 'But why in the world did not Hamlet obey the ghost at once, and so save seven of those eight lives?' And a highly unsympathetic aside of Mr. Eliot's converts Bradley's complaint at Hamlet's incompetence into a reproach to him for not being aware, as we are, that he 'has made a pretty considerable mess of things'. Mr. Eliot's rebuke to Hamlet for 'dying fairly well pleased with himself'[1] is only logical from a severe moralist if we accept that what the play has shown us is the mess which Hamlet has made of things. Mr. Eliot might, however, have noticed that it is not merely Hamlet who appears to feel at the close that if only the whole truth were known—as we, the audience, know it—the name which he leaves behind him would not be 'a wounded name'. Horatio's farewell to him and Fortinbras's comment make no suggestion that what we have witnessed is a story of personal failure and inadequacy; and Horatio's summary of what he will tell 'the yet unknowing world' does not include any hint that these things have come about through the bungling of the dead Prince. No need of extenuation appears to be felt. On the contrary, the play ends with 'the soldiers' music and the rites of war' and a final volley in salute of a dead hero.

The question here, which arises out of the play itself, is how we are to find consistency between the fact of Hamlet's

[1] 'Even Hamlet, who has made a pretty considerable mess of things, and occasioned the death of at least three innocent people, and two more insignificant ones, dies fairly well pleased with himself' ('Shakespeare and the Stoicism of Seneca', *Selected Essays*, 1932). The odd distinction between the innocent and the insignificant has already been commented on. Mr. Eliot's general complaint about the death-scenes of Elizabethan tragic heroes, whose *apologias* he ascribes to the influence of Seneca, ignores the historical fact that this was an age of public executions in which men were judged by the courage and dignity with which they met public death, and when it was thought proper that at this supreme moment of their lives they should submit their case to the judgement of their fellow-men. The best comment on Othello's last speech and Hamlet's entrusting of his cause to Horatio is provided by Sidney's Musidorus and Pyrocles in their condemned cell: 'In this time, place and fortune, it is lawfull for us to speak gloriously.'

delay, with which he bitterly reproaches himself, the fact, which Johnson pointed out, that the final denouement is not of his making, and the tone of the close of the play, which suggests so strongly that Hamlet has 'parted well and paid his score'. It hardly seems possible to answer this question, as Mr. Eliot does, by ascribing to Hamlet at the moment of his death, and by implication to his creator, a moral sensibility inferior to our own. When faced with a contradiction of this kind, the critic is bound to ask himself whether he has got the play out of focus. Is there some element in it which he is unaware of, which will, when perceived, make the close seem a full and fitting close? He needs to discover whether there is any means by which he can decide whether Shakespeare intended his audience to regard Hamlet as having 'made a mess of things'. And he must ask himself whether what Johnson thought an objection to the conduct of the plot, that the hero does so little to forward it, is a real objection: whether it does actually affect the 'satisfaction' which Johnson thought we should feel at the close of the play. The historical fact to which we can turn is that Shakespeare did not invent the plot of *Hamlet*. He chose, presumably because it in some way appealed to his imagination, to remake an older play. And, although this older play no longer exists, there exist other plays on the same kind of subject. A study of these, to see what they have in common with *Hamlet*, may, at the least, suggest to us things which we should take into account in trying to understand the masterpiece which Shakespeare created in this genre. Such a study shows that the answer which Bradley gave to his question 'Why in the world did not Hamlet obey the ghost at once?' is only a partial answer.

To Bradley's assertion, 'The whole story turns upon the peculiar character of the hero', we can object that heroes of very different character also fail to act promptly and also involve themselves and others in the final catastrophe. As for Johnson's comment on the conduct of the plot, we 'can say that the same complaint can be made to some degree against the plots of other revenge tragedies in the period. What Johnson thought to be a weakness in the plot of *Hamlet* appears to be a feature of the plots of other plays of the same kind and may point us towards a reason for their popularity and even towards what attracted Shakespeare in the old play which he re-made.

The essence of any tragedy of revenge is that its hero has not created the situation in which he finds himself and out of which the tragedy arises. The simplest of all tragic formulas, that a tragedy begins in prosperity and ends in misery, does not fit revenge tragedies. When the action opens the hero is seen in a situation which is horrible, and felt by him and the audience to be intolerable, but for which he has no responsibility. The exposition of such plays does not display the hero taking a fatal step, but the hero confronted with appalling facts. This is as true in Argos as it is in Denmark. But in Elizabethan revenge plays it is not merely the initial situation which is created by the villain. The denouement also comes about through his initiative. It is not the result of a successfully carried out scheme of the revenger. The revenger takes an opportunity unconsciously provided for him by the villain. Given this opportunity, which he seems unable to create for himself, he forms his scheme on the spur of the moment. Thus, in *The Spanish Tragedy*, Lorenzo, believing himself safe and that the secret of Horatio's murder lies buried with Serberine and Pedringano, feigns reconcilement with Hieronymo and invites him to provide a play for the entertainment of the court. By means of this play Hieronymo achieves his vengeance and brings to light the secret crime of Lorenzo. Similarly, in *Titus Andronicus*, which is obviously modelled on *The Spanish Tragedy*, although it exceeds it in horrors, the denouement comes about because Tamora believes she can deal with the old mad Titus and, through him, with his dangerous son Lucius who threatens her and her husband, the Emperor. Confident in her scheme, she delivers herself and her sons into Titus' hands. Up to the point when she calls upon him, disguised as Revenge, Titus has done nothing but indulge in wild gestures of grief and distraction; just as Hieronymo has done nothing to avenge his son before Lorenzo's initiative suggests to him a way of destroying his enemies and revealing their wickedness. Again, in a play written after *Hamlet*, Tourneur's *The Revenger's Tragedy*, the Duke himself asks Vendice, whose mistress he has poisoned because she would not yield to him, to find him a new mistress. He himself arranges the place, a hidden pavilion, and allows his courtiers to believe that he has gone away, so as to ensure secrecy. He thus provides Vendice with the perfect place and time for his vengeance. It seems as if in plays of this kind it was a necessary part of the total effect that the villain should be to some extent the agent of his own destruction. As initiator of the action he must be the initiator of its resolution. The satisfaction of the close included to a less or greater degree the sombre satisfaction which the Psalmist felt at the spectacle of the wicked falling into pits which they had digged for others.

Here, obscurely, the hand of heaven could be felt, as Raleigh felt it in the bloody pageant of history:

Oh by what plots, by what forswearings, betrayings, oppressions, imprisonments, tortures, poysonings, and under what reasons of State, and politique subtlety, have these forenamed Kings, both strangers, and of our owne Nation, pulled the vengeance of GOD upon themselves, upon theirs, and upon their prudent ministers! and in the end have brought those things to passe for their enemies, and seene an effect so directly contrary to all their owne counsels and cruelties, as the one could never have hoped for themselves, and the other never have succeeded, if no such opposition had ever been made. GOD hath said it and performed it ever: *Perdam sapientiam sapientium; I will destroy the wisedome of the wise.*[1]

'In the end' the wicked will destroy themselves and 'purposes mistook' will fall on 'the inventors' heads'. The hero waits for his opponent, as if for a signal, and the initiative and activity which Johnson expected from the hero of a play seems not to have been required from heroes in situations of this kind. This conception of a hero who is committed to counter-action, and to response to events rather than to the creation of events, is very powerfully rendered by Tourneur in the exposition of *The Revenger's Tragedy*. The personages of court pass across the stage, while Vendice, holding in his hands the skull of his dead mistress, comments on the parade of vicious power and wealth. He is waiting for 'that bald Madam, Opportunity'.

When we turn back from reading these plays to *Hamlet* we see that Shakespeare has very greatly developed this basic element in the revenge play of his day. He has developed it to make clear what in them is confused by sensationalism, and by that moral indignation which so easily converts itself to

[1] Preface to *The History of the World*, 1614.

immorality. Great writers perceive what is only half perceived by their lesser contemporaries and express what in them finds only partial or imperfect expression. In other revenge plays, once the signal is given, the revenger produces a scheme of horror by which he destroys his opponent. He becomes an agent, bent on fulfilling the hateful Senecan maxim that crimes are only to be avenged by greater crimes. The irony is only mild. It is ironic that the villain, acting as if all were well, invites his destroyer to destroy him. Once invited, the hero descends with alacrity to the moral level of his opponent. The vengeance when it comes is as hideous as the original crime, or even more hideous, and the moral feelings of the audience are confused between satisfaction and outrage.[1] In the denouement of *Hamlet* the irony is profound. Claudius, who has arranged the whole performance in order to destroy Hamlet, is himself destroyed and destroys his Queen. He is 'hoist with his own petard'. His tool Laertes acknowledges the justice of his fate as he reveals the plot to which he had consented: 'I am justly killed with mine own treachery.' Claudius himself makes no such acknowledgement. He dies impenitent; there is 'no relish of salvation' in his death. Kyd, with Hieronymo left alive on his hands at the end of the general holocaust, was forced to the weak expedient of making him commit suicide as the only way to preserve any sympathy for him. Hamlet

---

[1] It has been suggested by F. T. Bowers (*Elizabethan Revenge Tragedy*, 1940) that we are intended to lose sympathy with Hieronymo when, ignoring the command 'Vengeance is mine', he turns to plots himself and undertakes his murderous play. But the final speech of the Ghost makes it quite clear that to Kyd the characters remained to the end divided into sheep and goats. 'Good Hieronymo slaine by himselfe' is to be conducted with the innocent Isabella and his accomplice Bel-Imperia to the Elysian fields, while the rest of the cast are to be haled off to Tartarean regions by Revenge.

dies as a victim to that constancy to his purposes which has made him 'follow the king's pleasure' throughout. The end comes because he has accepted every challenge: 'If his fitness speaks, mine is ready.' Unlike Hieronymo, Titus, and Vendice, he remains to the last, in his adversary's words, 'most generous, and free from all contriving'. For there is another point in which an Elizabethan tragedy of revenge differs from the legend of Orestes and from the original Hamlet legend. Everyone in Argos is perfectly well aware that Clytemnestra, with the help of her paramour, Aegisthus, murdered her husband, Agamemnon, just as in the old story of Hamlet everyone knows that his uncle Feng is the murderer of his father. In these ancient stories of revenge for blood the criminals are known to be criminals by all their world. They are not 'secret men of blood'. The secrecy with which Kyd invests the murder of Horatio is carried to such fantastic lengths that at one point in the play it appears that the world in general does not even realize that he is dead. In *Hamlet*, as we know it, whether it was so in the old play or not, only his murderer among living men knows at the beginning of the action that Hamlet the elder was murdered. *The Spanish Tragedy* is built on a powerful moral contrast between the treacherous, subtle, politic Lorenzo and the honest man, Hieronymo, who lives by conscience and the law. At the crisis of the play this contrast is blurred and Hieronymo becomes as crafty as his enemy. In *Hamlet* it is preserved to the end, and Hamlet himself is far more of an instrument and far less of an agent than are his fellow revengers.

The view that the revenger's role was essentially a waiting role, that he was committed by the situation in which he found

himself to counter-action, and differentiated from his opponent by lack of guile, does not answer the question 'Why does
Hamlet delay?' It sets it in a different light. We must still find
consistency between his character and his actions, and Bradley's statement that 'the whole story turns on the peculiar
character of the hero' retains its truth. But to set *Hamlet*
against other plays of its time which handle the same kind of
subject is to suggest that however much he may reproach
himself with his delay, that delay is part of a pattern which is
made clear at the close. To ask 'Why in the world did not
Hamlet act at once?' is to fail to grasp the nature of the dilemma
which Kyd crudely adumbrated when he set the man of
conscience and duty against the conscienceless and treacherous
villain. Hamlet's agony of mind and indecision are precisely
the things which differentiate him from that smooth, swift
plotter Claudius, and from the coarse, unthinking Laertes,
ready to 'dare damnation' and cut his enemy's throat in a
churchyard. He quickly learns from Claudius how to entrap
the unwary and the generous, and betters the instruction. 'He
will never have a better opportunity', say many critics, when
Hamlet, convinced of his uncle's guilt and hot for vengeance,
comes on Claudius on his knees. Even Browning's ruthless
tyrant, after having long schemed his enemy's destruction,
shrank back and 'was afraid' when his victim 'caught at God's
skirts and prayed'. Do we really want to see Hamlet stab a
defenceless, kneeling man? This 'opportunity' is no opportunity at all; the enemy is within touching distance, but out of
reach. Hamlet's baffled rage finds an outlet in the speech
which shocked Johnson by its depth of hatred. The speech
reveals more than its speaker's character. Like many solilo-

quies, it is proleptic. The moment which Hamlet here declares that he will wait for, the real opportunity, will come. When Hamlet has gone and Claudius has risen from his knees, and not before, we know that Claudius has not found grace. The opportunity which Hamlet awaits Claudius will now provide. The play has made Hamlet certain of his uncle's guilt; it has also shown Claudius that his guilt is no longer his own secret. If he cannot repent, he must, for his own safety, destroy Hamlet. He will do it in his own characteristic way, by the hand of an accomplice and by the treacherous man's characteristic weapon, poison. And Hamlet will destroy Claudius in his own characteristic way also: by 'rashness' and 'indiscretion', and not by 'deep plots'. He will catch him at the moment when his guilt has been made clear to all the bystanders, so that as he runs the sword through him he will do so not as an assassin but as an executioner. The dark and devious world in which Hamlet finds himself, when he accepts the necessity of obeying the command of the Ghost, involves all who enter it in guilt. But Hamlet's most terrible deed, when he allows himself to be 'marshalled to knavery' and is most contaminated by his world, the sending of the traitors Rosencrantz and Guildenstern to their deaths, is a spontaneous, savage response to the discovery of their treachery; and his other crime, the killing of Polonius, with its consequence in the madness and death of Ophelia, is also unpremeditated.

In *Othello*, Iago, speaking in the role of an honest man, puts crudely to his master the code of a soldier:

> Though in the trade of war I have slain men,
> Yet do I hold it very stuff o' the conscience
> To do no contriv'd murder.

Hamlet is fittingly borne 'like a soldier, to the stage', because in the secret war which he has waged he has shown a soldier's virtues. Pre-eminently he has shown the virtue of constancy. He has not laid down his arms and quitted the field. For Bradley's comment, 'Two months have passed and he has done nothing', we might better say, 'Two months have passed and he is still there, at his post, on guard.' The play ends with a soldier's funeral. It opens with sentries at their watch, being relieved. In his four great tragedies, when his imagination was working at its highest pitch, Shakespeare relates his beginnings to his ends particularly closely. Granville Barker pointed out how *King Lear* ends as it began with Lear and his three daughters on the stage and with the old king hanging on the hope of words from Cordelia's lips. Any writer dramatizing Cinthio's story of the Moor of Venice would end with the midnight scenes of the attempted murder of Cassio and the death of Desdemona. Shakespeare has invented a great midnight opening to balance this close, with brawling in the streets followed by the midnight scene before the Senate, where, with the approval of Venice, Othello is united to Desdemona, as in the last scene he is united to her in death before the eyes of the envoys of Venice. *Macbeth* begins and ends with battles. It opens with the epic narrative of the defeat of the thane of Cawdor who had rebelled, and closes with the defeat of the thane of Cawdor who had usurped. And here there is contrast. The first thane confessed his treasons 'very freely' and died well, giving up his life, 'the dearest thing he owed', 'as 'twere a trifle': his successor in the title, Macbeth, fought desperately to the last to preserve a life which had become meaningless to him. The opening and the close of

Hamlet have the same kind of relation to each other. The soldier on guard, who cannot leave his post until he is relieved or given permission from above, is a metaphor for the soul in this world which comes very easily to Renaissance writers. Its source is Cicero's gloss on the 'secret doctrine' which Socrates appealed to in his argument against suicide in the *Phaedo*.[1] The Red Cross Knight uses it against Despair:

> The souldier may not move from watchfull sted
> Nor leave his stand, untill his Captain bed.

And Donne, speaking of this world as 'the appointed field', refers to the same commonplace when he chides the 'desperate coward' who yields to the foes of him

> who made thee to stand
> Sentinell in his worlds garrison.

The play of *Hamlet* continually recurs to the thought of suicide, and the temptation to give up the battle of life. Hamlet's first soliloquy opens with the lament that the Almighty has 'fixed his canon 'gainst self-slaughter', and his last action is to snatch the poisoned cup from the lips of Horatio. Within this frame of soldiers on the watch, being relieved, and of a soldier's laying to rest, I do not believe that the Elizabethans thought that they were witnessing a story of personal failure. Nor do I think that we should do so either, unless we are certain of what, in this situation, would be success.

The tragedy of *Hamlet*, and of plays of its kind, of which

---

[1] 'Vetat Pythagoras injussu imperatoris, id est dei, de praesidio et statione vitae decedere' (*De Senectute*, 20); cf. *Phaedo*, 62.

it is the supreme example, does not lie in 'the unfitness of the hero for his task', or in some 'fatal flaw'. It is not true that a coarser nature could have cleansed the state of Denmark, some 'Hotspur of the North': 'he that kills me some six or seven of Scots at a breakfast, washes his hands, and says to his wife, "Fie upon this quiet life! I want work."' The tragedy lies in the nature of the task, which only the noble will feel called on to undertake, or rather, in the nature of the world which is exposed to the hero's contemplation and in his sense of responsibility to the world in which he finds himself. *Hamlet* towers above other plays of its kind through the heroism and nobility of its hero, his superior power of insight into, and reflection upon, his situation, and his capacity to suffer the moral anguish which moral responsibility brings. Hamlet is the quintessence of European man, who holds that man is 'ordained to govern the world according to equity and righteousness with an upright heart', and not to renounce the world and leave it to its corruption. By that conception of man's duty and destiny he is involved in those tragic dilemmas with which our own age is so terribly familiar. For how can man secure justice except by committing injustice, and how can he act without outraging the very conscience which demands that he should act?

It will have been apparent for some time that I am coming round to a point where I am demonstrating the historical nature of my own answer to my question. Although I have gone to the Elizabethans to ask how *Hamlet* appeared to audiences which had applauded *The Spanish Tragedy* and *Titus Andronicus*, it is the moral uncertainties and the moral dilemmas of my own age which make me unable to see *Hamlet* in terms of the hero's failure or success in the task which the Ghost lays upon him.

> For this same lord,
> I do repent: but heaven hath pleas'd it so,
> To punish me with this, and this with me,
> That I must be their scourge and minister.

Hamlet, speaking over the body of one of his victims, Polonius, speaks for all those called on to attempt to secure justice, the supporters of 'just wars' as well as those who fight in them. In trying to set *Hamlet* back into its own age, I seem to have found in it an image of my own time. The Elizabethan Hamlet assumes the look of the Hamlet of the twentieth century.

That the answers we find are conditioned by our own circumstances does not destroy their value. *Hamlet* is not a problem to which a final solution exists. It is a work of art about which questions can always be asked. Each generation asks its own questions and finds its own answers, and the final test of the validity of those answers can only be time. Johnson, Coleridge, Bradley, all tell us things about *Hamlet* which are consistent with the play as we read it. A critic today cannot hope for more than that his questions and answers will seem relevant, and will continue to seem relevant, to others who read and ponder the play. The reward of the historical approach is not that it leads us to a final and infallible interpretation.

III

INTERPRETATION

THE counterpoise to the necessity of 'examining the genius of his age and the opinions of his contemporaries', if we are to arrive at 'a just estimate' of a writer's quality and to understand his meaning, is the necessity of learning the author's own personal language, the idiom of his thought. The discipline of imaginative intercourse is not wholly different from the discipline of social intercourse. We learn to know our friends so that we do not misunderstand them, or put a wrong construction on their actions. We can say with certainty, 'He can't have meant that', because we know the kind of person 'he' is. In the same kind of way we can arrive at a similar conviction about a poem because we know the habit of an author's mind and are familiar with his associations of ideas and have come to sympathize with his moral temper. It is possible, in the light of this knowledge, to check our own habits and associations and feel some assurance that one interpretation is better, because more characteristic, than another.

Like the historical sense, this sense of a writer's individual habit of mind is no infallible guide. We cannot tie an author down to repeating himself any more than we can tie him to saying what his contemporaries say. Within the range of a temperament we often meet with surprises. If an author is prevailingly serious, we must not insist that he can never be jocose, and because we cannot find any parallel in his works we cannot, therefore, insist that he cannot mean in one work what he must mean there, if the work is to make sense. If it is a passage which we are interpreting, the final test is always the consistency of the interpretation of the passage with the interpretation of the work as a whole. If we are attempting the interpretation of a single complete work, the test is the reverse of this: does our interpretation of the whole make sense of all the parts?

A good example of the necessity of disciplining our imaginations and our responses by asking what associations the poet had in mind, rather than using the author's words as a starting-point for associations of our own, is a passage in *Macbeth* which was interpreted at some length by Professor Cleanth Brooks in *The Well-Wrought Urn* (1947). It can be shown that the critic has distorted the sense of the passage to make it an example of his general theory of the nature of poetry as distinct from prose. The interpretation he gives is shallower and less in keeping with the play as a whole than the interpretation we can arrive at by using Shakespeare to comment on Shakespeare. He isolates for discussion the lines where Macbeth 'compares the pity for his victim-to-be, Duncan', to

> a naked new-born babe,
> Striding the blast, or heaven's cherubin, hors'd
> Upon the sightless couriers of the air . . .

and he comments as follows:

The comparison is odd, to say the least. Is the babe natural or supernatural—an ordinary helpless baby, who, as newborn, could not, of course, even toddle, much less stride the blast? Or is it some infant Hercules, quite capable of striding the blast, but, since it is powerful and not helpless, hardly the typical pitiable object?

Shakespeare seems bent upon having it both ways—and, if we read on through the passage—bent upon having the best of both worlds; for he proceeds to give us the option: pity is like the babe 'or heaven's cherubim' who quite appropriately, of course, do ride the blast. Yet, even if we waive the question of the legitimacy of the alternative ... is the cherubim comparison really any more successful than is the babe comparison? Would not one of the great warrior archangels be more appropriate to the scene than the cherub? Does Shakespeare mean for pity or for fear of retribution to be dominant in Macbeth's mind?

Or was it possible that Shakespeare could not make up his own mind? Was he merely writing hastily and loosely, letting the word 'pity' suggest the typically pitiable object, the babe naked in the blast, and then, stirred by the vague notion that some threat to Macbeth should be hinted, using 'heaven's cherubim'—already suggested by 'babe'—to convey the hint?

We know what the answer will be to all this puzzlement.[1] Shakespeare 'meant for both'. The passage is an example of the ambiguity, irony, paradox—the terms are roughly interchangeable—which Professor Brooks holds to be the differentiating quality of poetic speech. Later in the same essay the meaning is revealed:

Pity is like the naked babe, the most sensitive and helpless thing, yet almost as soon as the comparison is announced, the symbol of weakness begins to turn into a symbol of strength; for the babe, though newborn, is pictured as 'Striding the blast' like an elemental

[1] It is a part of the game of 'explication', as it has developed, to begin by expressing complete bafflement, as if the critic had never met a metaphor in his life. Then after every kind of obtuseness has been exhibited and all possible interpretations and misinterpretations have been considered, the true explication rises like the sun out of foggy mists.

force—like 'heaven's cherubim'. . . . We can give an answer to the question put earlier: is Pity like the human and helpless babe, or powerful as the angel that rides the winds? It is both. . . . The final and climactic appearance of the babe symbol merges all the contradictory elements of the symbol. For, with Macduff's statement about his birth, the naked babe rises before Macbeth as not only the future that eludes calculation but as avenging angel as well.

But why does Professor Brooks think that 'heaven's cherubim' 'quite appropriately ride the blast'? Why are they any more suitably imagined as 'horsed' than the naked babe as 'striding'? Why is it to be assumed that they imply 'some threat to Macbeth'? Are cherubim to be thought of as powerful? Have we any reason to suppose that they should at once suggest to us the cliché 'avenging angel'?

Most editors rightly cite here Psalm xviii, where the Lord is described descending in judgement: 'He bowed the heavens also and came down: and it was dark under his feet. He rode upon the cherubims and did fly: he came flying upon the wings of the wind.' Similarly, in Ezekiel's vision the cherubim are between the wheels of the chariot of the Lord; for the cherubim, in the visions of the Old Testament, are the glory of the Lord, the signs of his presence. I do not doubt that the association 'cherubims'—'wings of the wind' helped to create Shakespeare's lines. But there is no suggestion in the psalm, although it is a psalm of judgement, that cherubim are avenging angels. It is the Lord who is borne up by the cherubim; it is he that flies on the wings of the wind. The cherubim are among the higher orders of angels—the ministers who stand about the throne. They are not the executors of God's purposes. They are with the Lord, whether he comes in mercy or in judgement: 'The Lord is King be the people never so unpatient; he sitteth between the cherubims be the earth never so unquiet.' The cherubim, all gold and gilded over, carved at the two ends of the mercy-seat, in the description of the covenant in Exodus, are the tokens of the presence of the Lord among his people.

These are the cherubim of the Old Testament. Dionysius the Areopagite, who established the hierarchy of the angels, the source of the popular angelology of the Middle Ages, which the Elizabethans inherited, ranked the cherubim among the higher orders, as angels of the presence. They stood about the throne, contemplating the glory of God, not active, as were the lower orders, to fulfil his will on earth. The cherubim glowed with knowledge, as the seraphim burned with love. Hamlet, a scholarly character, glances at this learned conception of the cherubim in his retort to Claudius:

> *Claudius.* So is it, if thou knew'st our purposes.
> *Hamlet.* I see a cherub that sees them.

Elsewhere, apart from two references to the gilded carvings of cherubim, Shakespeare appears to use the word in its popular sense, to signify primarily beauty, particularly the radiant and innocent beauty of youth. Thus we may have the word used, as in Sonnet 114, for a simple opposite to the hideous:

> To make of monsters and things indigest
> Such cherubins as your sweet self resemble.

Or the idea of youthfulness is stressed, as in *The Merchant of Venice*:

> Still quiring to the young-eyed cherubins

or the idea of innocence, as in *Timon of Athens*:

> This fell whore of thine
> Hath in her more destruction than thy sword
> For all her cherubin look.

But in two plays, one written just before, the other some time after *Macbeth*, Shakespeare gives this innocent youthful beauty a certain moral colouring which is, as far as I know, his own; at least I have not met with it in another writer. In the late play, *The Tempest*, Prospero tells Miranda how he was set adrift with her when she was a baby, and she exclaims

> Alack! what trouble
> Was I then to you.

But he answers:

> O, a cherubin
> Thou wast, that did preserve me! Thou didst smile,
> Infused with a fortitude from heaven,
> When I have deck'd the sea with drops full salt,
> Under my burden groan'd; which rais'd in me
> An undergoing stomach, to bear up
> Against what should ensue.

Because Prospero sees the three-year-old Miranda as a cherub, smiling and giving him patience to bear up, I find no difficulty in taking Othello's cry 'Patience, thou young and rose-lipped cherubin!' as an apostrophe to a virtue which Shakespeare elsewhere pictures as radiantly young and beautiful. In the recognition scene of *Pericles*, Pericles, gazing on his exquisite young daughter, who claims that she has endured 'a grief might equal yours', wonders at her endurance, for, he exclaims,

> thou dost look
> Like Patience gazing on kings' graves, and smiling
> Extremity out of act.

Although Viola's description of her sister, 'like Patience on a monument, smiling at grief', is often cited to prove that Shakespeare could not have thought of Patience as 'young and rose-lipped', since Viola's sister had lost her damask cheek and had pined in thought,[1] the passage in *Pericles* admits of no doubt. It plainly implies a beauty untouched by care. In *Othello* then, written just before *Macbeth*, and in *The Tempest*, written some time after, a cherub is thought of as not only young, beautiful, and innocent, but as associated with the virtue of patience, conceived of as an endurance which is not grim, but heavenly, smiling, and serene. It could, however, be objected at this point that because Shakespeare elsewhere invariably sees the cherubim as young and beautiful, and conceives them as particularly associated with the bearing of wrong rather than with the avenging of it, we cannot assume that he never saw them otherwise. Although there is no support for the idea in Scripture or in popular angelology, and no parallel elsewhere in his works, he might, in this passage, because of a confused memory of Psalm xviii, conceive

---

[1] This is absurdly supported by some commentators by reference to Nym's 'Patience is a tired nag.' There has been much discussion as to whether Shakespeare had a particular monument in mind. Although none has been discovered to fit the description, I think, in spite of their being far apart in time, we must take both Viola's and Pericles' words as referring to the same conception. Because Viola's sister lost her beauty, we need not take it that Shakespeare means us to think of the virtue which she exemplifies as pale and worn. She is like Patience on a monument in that she 'smiles at grief'.

of cherubim as avengers threatening Macbeth; for there is
apocalyptic imagery just before in the simile of the accusing
'angels trumpet-tongu'd'.

The context is our final test. Macbeth, having acknowledged
the certainty of retribution in this life, that 'we still have
judgement here', goes on to give the reasons which make the
deed which he is meditating peculiarly base. It is the murder
of a kinsman and a king, who is also a guest who trusts his
host to protect him:

> Besides, this Duncan
> Hath borne his faculties so meek, hath been
> So clear in his great office, that his virtues
> Will plead like angels trumpet-tongu'd against
> The deep damnation of his taking off;
> And pity, like a naked new-born babe,
> Striding the blast, or heaven's cherubin, hors'd
> Upon the sightless couriers of the air,
> Shall blow the horrid deed in every eye,
> That tears shall drown the wind.

The final image of the wind dropping as the rain begins is the
termination of the whole sequence of ideas and images. It is to
this close that they hurry. The passage ends with tears stilling
the blast. The final condemnation of the deed is not that it will
meet with punishment, not even that the doer of it will stand
condemned; but that even indignation at the murder will be
swallowed up in universal pity for the victim. The whole
world will know, and knowing it will not curse but weep.
The babe, naked and new-born, the most helpless of all
things, the cherubim, innocent and beautiful, call out the pity
and the love by which Macbeth is judged. It is not terror of
heaven's vengeance which makes him pause; but the terror of

moral isolation. He ends by seeing himself alone in a sudden silence, where nothing can be heard but weeping, as, when a storm has blown itself out, the wind drops and we hear the steady falling of the rain, which sounds as if it would go on for ever. The naked babe 'strides the blast' because pity is to Shakespeare the strongest and profoundest of human emotions, the distinctively human emotion. It rises above and masters indignation. The cherubim are borne with incredible swiftness about the world because the virtues of Duncan are of such heavenly beauty that they command universal love and reverence. He has 'borne his faculties so meek' and been 'so clear in his great office'. The word 'clear' is a radiant word, used by Shakespeare elsewhere of the Gods. The helplessness of the king who has trusted him, his gentle virtues, and patient goodness are transformed in Macbeth's mind into the most helpless of all things, what most demands our protection, and then into what awake tenderness, love, and reverence. The babe merges into the cherubim, not because Shakespeare means Macbeth to be feeling both pity and fear of retribution at the same time, but because Shakespeare, like Keats, believes in 'the holiness of the heart's affections'.

In a very early play, in a savage scene full of curses and cries for vengeance, Shakespeare uses the same natural image as he does here. In Henry VI, part 3, Margaret, having crowned York with a paper crown, hands him a napkin dipped in his little son's blood, and York exclaims

> Bidd'st thou me rage? why, now thou hast thy wish;
> Would'st have me weep? why, now thou hast thy will;
> For raging wind blows up incessant showers,
> And when the rage allays, the rain begins.

And in his next speech he prophesies that Margaret's deed will have the same condemnation as Macbeth forsees for his:

> Keep thou the napkin, and go boast of this;
> And if thou tell'st the heavy story right,
> Upon my soul, the hearers will shed tears;
> Yea, even my foes will shed fast-falling tears,
> And say, 'Alas! it was a piteous deed.'

This seems feeble enough, and yet it holds the characteristic Shakespearian appeal to our deepest moral feelings. The worst suffering is to suffer alone; it is more comfort to York in his agony to think that common humanity will make even his enemies weep with him than to think of vengeance on the murderess of his son. Professor Brooks has sacrificed this Shakespearian depth of human feeling, visible even in this crude early play, by attempting to interpret an image by the aid of what associations it happens to arouse in him, and by being more interested in making symbols of babes fit each other than in listening to what Macbeth is saying. *Macbeth* is a tragedy and not a melodrama or a symbolic drama of retribution. The reappearance of 'the babe symbol' in the apparition scene and in Macduff's revelation of his birth has distracted the critic's attention from what deeply moves the imagination and the conscience in this vision of a whole world weeping at the inhumanity of helplessness betrayed and innocence and beauty destroyed. It is the judgement of the human heart that Macbeth fears here, and the punishment which the speech foreshadows is not that he will be cut down by Macduff, but that having murdered his own humanity he will enter into a world of appalling loneliness, of meaningless activity, unloved himself, and unable to love.

Asking the relevant historical questions and trying to learn a writer's language are means to an end. They subserve the aim of discovering the peculiar virtue of the individual work, play, poem, or novel. This means recognizing its true subject, or imaginative centre, the source of the work's unity and of its whole tone. If we do not thus recognize the subject, feel the unity, and respond to the tone, we have not understood what we have read, or else the work is unsatisfying in itself; but this is a decision we cannot come to quickly. We need to be certain that the fault is not in our eyes, but is in the writer's failure to achieve a fully coherent and expressive work of art. I am going to show what I mean negatively by discussing a poem whose peculiar virtue I do not feel certain that I have grasped, although the relevant historical questions are easily answered and I have some familiarity with the author's habits of mind and language: the poem of Donne's which goes under the title of 'Air and Angels'.[1]

The obsolete idea which Donne makes use of in this poem is easily explained. The Schoolmen, holding angels to be spiritual beings, but believing, on the testimony of Scripture, that angels had on many occasions appeared in visible form to men, had to explain what it was that men saw when they saw angels, what 'bodies' angels wore, or assumed, when they appeared on earth. All matter consisted of the four elements. Since angels appeared suddenly, and as suddenly vanished, without leaving a trace, their bodies could not be framed of earth or water. Nor could they make use of the element of fire, since if they did they would burn all they touched; nor could they use air, since air is invisible. The way out of this

[1] *The Poems of John Donne*, edited by H. J. C. Grierson, 2 vols., 1912, i. 22.

logical impasse was to postulate that the bodies which angels assumed were of air, but air condensed to cloud, which could at will be uncondensed and vanish. The difficulty of the poem does not lie here. Nor is there any real difficulty in following its argument, once we recognize the theological flavour of the language and if we use other poems by Donne to help us, particularly a song called 'Negative Love' and the more famous 'Love's Deity'.

In 'Negative Love' Donne declares that he does not know what it is that he loves:

> I never stoop'd so low, as they
> Which on an eye, cheeke, lip, can prey,
>> Seldome to them, which soare no higher
>> Then vertue or the minde to admire,
> For sense, and understanding may
>> Know, what gives fuell to their fire:
> My love, though silly, is more brave,
> For may I misse, when ere I crave,
> If I know yet, what I would have.
>
> If that be simply perfectest
> Which can by no way be exprest
>> But *Negatives*, my love is so.
>> To All, which all love, I say no.
> If any who deciphers best
>> What we know not, our selves, can know,
> Let him teach mee that nothing; This
> As yet my ease, and comfort is,
> Though I speed not, I cannot misse.[1]

In this poem, one of the most purely delightful of Donne's lyrics, theological ideas, of course, are lurking: the doctrine that God, the absolute perfection, cannot be known and can

[1] Grierson, i. 66.

only be described negatively, since to attempt to define him by attributes is to limit his perfection, and the mystical doctrine that the way to know God is to know our own souls, the soul being a mirror in which we can see God spiritually. But these ideas are lightly touched on, not laboured, in a poem that makes its point perfectly. As in many of his poems, Donne declares that he is a special case. He distinguishes himself from the sensual lover and then from the spiritual; with a characteristic turn of wit he declares that he aims higher than these latter high-minded persons. What he loves is something divine and inexpressible, beyond what either the senses or the understanding can apprehend. If he could learn to know his own soul, he might know the 'nothing' which he loves; but anyhow he is saved from the disappointments of those who know what they want.

'Air and Angels' appears to be setting out to answer the question which 'Negative Love' so gaily declares to be unanswerable: what is it we love when we say we love another person? It is, unlike 'Negative Love', spoken to someone. But, unlike most of Donne's poems spoken to a woman, it is not spoken in a particular situation. It is a lecture in love's philosophy, not a dramatic lyric, or a persuasion. As we read the first stanza we are aware that we are not listening to the tone of song or the tone of drama, but to thet one of reflection and meditation:

> Twice or thrice had I loved thee,
> Before I knew thy face or name;
> So in a voice, so in a shapelesse flame,
> *Angells* affect us oft, and worship'd bee;
> Still when, to where thou wert, I came

Some lovely glorious nothing I did see.
　But since my soule, whose child love is,
Takes limmes of flesh, and else could nothing doe,
　More subtile then the parent is,
Love must not be, but take a body too,
　And therefore what thou wert, and who,
　　I bid Love aske, and now
That it assume thy body, I allow,
And fixe it selfe in thy lip, eye, and brow.

Donne opens his poem with a bold absurdity, a more startling
way of saying what he says in 'The Good-Morrow':

If ever any beauty I did see,
Which I desir'd, and got, t'was but a dreame of thee.

When he first saw his mistress he felt 'This is the person I
have loved before.' When he loved thus he did not know what
it was that he loved; he was conscious, that is to say, only of
a feeling of response in himself, as a man might respond to the
power of an unbodied angel, felt in a voice heard or a flash of
glory.[1] A 'shapelesse flame' is exact; he means not a steady
flame, but a sudden diffusion of fire and light, which comes
and goes in a flash and raises sensations of awe and worship of
an unknown power. A bitter poem, 'Farewell to Love', provides a comment on this ignorant awe:

　　　　　Whilst yet to prove,
I thought there was some Deitie in love,
So did I reverence, and gave
Worship; as Atheists at their dying houre
Call, what they cannot name, an unknowne power,
As ignorantly did I crave:[2]

[1] Cf. the proverb 'By this fire, that's God's angel'; see F. P. Wilson, 'Shakespeare and the Diction of Common Life', *Proceedings of the British Academy*,
1941, p. 184, for examples of the use of this saying.
[2] Grierson, i. 70.

He was conscious only of an effect, but could not define its cause. And when he first met her it was the same. He saw only 'some lovely glorious nothing'. This is love at first sight, or falling in love. It is one thing to fall in love; but what is it to 'be' in love? If love is to exist on earth, to 'be' in this world, it must accept the laws of natural existence. Being is the union of form and matter. As the human soul needs a body—for it is the union of soul and body which makes a man—so love, the child of the soul, must find a body, must incarnate itself, if it is to exist as an inhabitant of this earth. It cannot be more subtle and refined than its parent the soul, and operate as pure spirit. When love, a feeling in him, finds its proper object in her, then it will become something constant and take on a real existence in this world. The union of his love with what he loves in her he thinks of as something as close as the union of soul and body in a man. But what is love's proper object? He begins by recognizing a personality. He bids his love inquire 'what *thou* art and *who*'; and, because personality is known to us by physical accidents, he allows that his love should find its object first in her beauty of face. The first verse comes to a beautiful close as his desire anchors itself here. *My* love—the worship called out by the unknown cause—has become my *love*, the woman whom I love as a beautiful creature. He can now say, '*She* is my love.'

But the next stanza rejects this conclusion. Without its final three lines, it runs to another close:

> Whilst thus to ballast love, I thought,
> And so more steddily to have gone,
> With wares which would sinke admiration,
> I saw I had loves pinnace over fraught,

        Ev'ry thy haire for love to worke upon
    Is much too much, some fitter must be sought;
        For, nor in nothing, nor in things
    Extreme, and scatt'ring bright, can love inhere;
        Then as an Angell, face, and wings
    Of aire, not pure as it, yet pure doth weare
    So thy love may be my loves spheare. . . .

Changing his metaphor he thinks of his love now as a ship
loaded to make it sail more steadily; but he declares that he
has overloaded it. His little pinnace staggers and lurches;
wonder or admiration, which should be the beginning of
knowledge, sinks beneath too much to admire and is destroyed. Love is the child of the soul and it must find a body
like to itself, something which it does not assume but in
which it can inhere. Both words are theological in colour.
The word 'assume' is common for the taking of flesh by the
Son; but the word 'inhere' expresses another kind of relation,
the relation of spirit to spirit. It is used to express the relation
of the Persons of the Trinity within the Unity of the God-
head, or the relation of the saved to their Saviour. Love cannot inhere in nothing, nor in things, however beautiful. And
so he takes up again his first notion of angels affecting men,
and remembering the old debate on the nature of angelic
appearances finds in that the analogy he needs. An angel,
if it wishes to appear on earth, finds for its body the
material substance nearest to itself: the 'pure and serene
air' of the regions beyond the moon, the purest of material
substances, though not as pure as itself, since it is still
material, not spiritual. Man's love, also, must find for its
body what is nearest to it, the love of woman. When love

finds love, then love truly is. For, as Donne says in 'Love's Deity'[1]

> It cannot bee
> Love, till I love her, that loves mee.

Love is neither worship, nor love of the beloved's beauty, although these are, perhaps, necessary stages. If it is to be real it must be a relation between two persons loving, born of both. In this analogy Donne finds the 'Correspondencie' (the word he uses in 'Love's Deity'), the 'something fitter' which he has been seeking. Active here finds passive, form matter, soul body, and intelligence sphere. As the angel takes to itself a body of air, so man's love takes to itself woman's love; here it finds the sphere which, like an intelligence, or angel, it may direct and move.

> So thy love may be my loves spheare.

And then Donne adds

> Just such disparitie
> As is twixt Aire and Angells puritie,
> 'Twixt womens love, and mens will ever bee.

Here is the problem for the critic. Up to this point the poem has seemed to be a serious and uncynical, even idealistic, inquiry into the nature of love between men and women; and the woman has been paid hyperbolic compliments. Now, suddenly, the point seems to be that women are inferior to men. Are we to think that we have been conducted through these labyrinths to receive this slap in the face at the end? Many critics have taken the view that the end of the poem is an

[1] Grierson, i. 54.

intended anti-climax, and an attempt to justify it artistically has been made by Mr. Leonard Unger:

The lover addresses the woman he loves in terms of praise, until almost the end of the poem. And then it develops that this discussion leads to a statement that the woman is in a respect lower than the lover. With this surprising reversal, seemingly unprepared for, the poem ends. The reversal is surprising, and a calculated surprise is witty. Moreover, the reversal makes for irony: one attitude is apparently prepared for, and then its opposite is given. Hence the poem is not a straightforward development of a single attitude, but provides a complexity of attitudes.[1]

This seems to me a desperate position. We are asked to accept that Donne has written so tenderly, with such refinement of language, in order to deceive us and to shock us by a turn, which we have had no reason to anticipate, at the end. If this is a joke, it is a bad one. Calculated surprises are not necessarily witty. This sounds like the intellectual equivalent of pulling away a chair from under a person about to sit down, which has never been regarded as a very witty stroke. And it is no use pointing to other poems with shock endings, such as 'Woman's Constancy', because here the tone of calculated roughness at the beginning prepares us for the insult at the end. In 'Air and Angels' the tone of impassioned reverie and intellectual seriousness requires something better than a point scored off women. A surprise is only justified in art if, when it comes, we see that we should have expected it, and if it puts what has gone before in a fresh light. If Mr. Unger's interpretation is right and we are to accept the disappointment which many critics have felt in the last three lines as intended, then the poem is artistically trivial.

[1] *Donne's Poetry and Modern Criticism*, Chicago, 1950, p. 44.

Another explanation might be that Donne has failed to solve a formal difficulty. Professor Pierre Legouis pointed out long ago that Donne was often hard put to it, having created a complex opening stanza, to write a second stanza on the same model.[1] 'Air and Angels' is a good example of a poem whose first stanza is a finer musical whole than its second. Is the truth of the matter that Donne, having written a beautiful verse paragraph for his first stanza, finds himself at the end of his argument before he has come to the end of his stanza, and has been forced to fill up his self-created frame by adding three lines, which are really a kind of footnote to the argument? If this is so, we must regard the poem as not wholly successful, and this judgement on it would be a judgement by Donne's own standards. Although he is famous for his fine openings, he himself thought that a poem's force lay in its close, as he says in an aside in one of his sermons:

In all Metricall compositions, of which kinde the booke of Psalmes is, the force of the whole piece is for the most part left to the shutting up; the whole frame of the Poem is a beating out of a piece of gold, but the last clause is as the impression of the stamp, and that is it that makes it current.[2]

This warns us that in interpreting a poem by Donne we should pay special attention to its final clause, and if, as here, we find it to be a disappointment, then we must judge the poem to be imperfect.

But before deciding that the poem is a failure, we ought to be sure that we have not got it in some way out of focus. It does not sound as if it were spoken directly to a woman, who

[1] *Donne the Craftsman*, Paris, 1928.
[2] *LXXX Sermons*, 1640, no. 55, p. 549.

is first to feel flattered and then to find herself put in her place.
It sounds more like a meditation on love, not necessarily
spoken in the mistress's presence. We are not aware, as we
read, of the implied presence and implied reaction of another
person, as we are in such poems as the lively, argumentative
'The Flea' or the impassioned 'A Valediction of Weeping'.
Mr. Unger's interpretation asks us to regard this poem as
semi-dramatic. Is it, on the contrary, not a dramatic poem,
embodying a certain attitude, but a metaphysical poem in the
proper sense of the term, an attempt to consider the nature of
the relations of men and women in love. The ethereal body
of an angel, however rarified its substance may be, is still
material. It has not the absolute purity of spirit, which alone
is incorruptible and indestructible, absolutely simple and un-
mixed. Perhaps Donne feels that the truth of his analogy is
confirmed by its congruence with his general conception of
woman as unlike man and, since she is not superior, inferior. It
is possible that there is no shock at all in the last three lines
and that Donne is, on the contrary, appealing to a generally
accepted idea to prove that he has found a fit comparison.

One has only to turn to such an impeccably orthodox
source as the Homily 'Of the State of Matrimonie', first published in the *Second Book of Homilies* in 1563, to see that the
idea of woman as the 'weaker vessel' was not held only by
satirists:

For the woman is a weake creature, not indued with like strength
and constancy of minde, therefore they bee the sooner disquieted,
and they bee the more prone to all weake affections and dispositions
of minde, more then men bee, and lighter they bee, and more vaine
in their fantisies and opinions.

This is the orthodox view of women, put kindly. Duke Orsino explains more candidly what is meant by the Homily's references to women's 'frail hearts'.

> There is no woman's sides
> Can bide the beating of so strong a passion
> As love doth give my heart: no woman's heart
> So big, to hold so much; they lack retention.
> Alas! their love may be call'd appetite,
> No motion of the liver, but the palate,
> That suffers surfeit, cloyment and revolt.

Shakespeare, by the light of his uncommon common sense, not so well read in Aristotle and scholastic philosophy as Donne, allows Viola by the story of her sister and by her own example to rebut this piece of male complacency. But Shakespeare is a much more original writer than Donne. Still, Donne is not being nearly as insulting to women's love as Duke Orsino. He is saying that there is only so much difference between man's and woman's love as there is between pure spirit and the thing which is nearest to it, the pure air of the heavens. And we are not asked, in Donne's context, to give 'pure' an ethical connotation. We are being asked to see the love of woman as 'not pure spirit', but mixed. And we may agree that there is some sense in this. Woman has more reason to feel fear in love than man has, and can never, perhaps, be so single-minded. When the lady in 'The Dream' rises to go, her disappointed lover exclaims:

> That love is weake, where feare's as strong as hee;
> 'Tis not all spirit, pure, and brave,
> If mixture it of *Feare, Shame, Honor,* have.[1]

Some mixture of feeling is perhaps always present in a woman.

[1] Grierson, i. 37.

However this may be, even the most ardent Platonists were forced, if they tried to relate their doctrine to current conceptions of the nature of things, to face the implication of the unquestioned assumption that the active, or masculine principle is superior to the passive, or feminine. Thus the lover, Philo, speaking to his mistress, Sophia, in Leone Ebreo's *Dialoghi d'Amore*,[1] a book which I am convinced Donne knew well, has to apologize to her for making this very point. 'Which is the truer and more unalloyed love,' asks Sophia, 'that of superior for inferior or that of inferior for superior?' And Philo replies:

> That of superior for inferior and of spirit for matter. . . . Because the one is of receiving, the other of giving. The superior spirit loves the inferior as a father his child, and the inferior loves the superior as a child its father: and you know how much more perfect is paternal love than filial. Again the spiritual loves the corporeal world as a man loves a woman, and the corporeal loves the spiritual world as woman loves man. . . . Suffer me to say, O Sophia, that the love of man, who gives, is more perfect than that of woman, who receives.

In the light of the all-pervading belief that the word 'masculine' means 'perfect', and the word 'feminine' means 'imperfect',[2] Donne's closing statement loses its sting. We should

---

[1] Written 1501–2 and published at Rome in 1535 and at Venice in 1541 and 1545. It was twice translated into French and three times into Spanish as well as into Latin and Hebrew. The quotation is from the translation by F. Friede-berg-Seeley and Jean H. Barnes under the title *The Philosophy of Love*, 1937, pp. 180–1.

[2] Spenser, who can hardly be accused of holding a low view of woman, accepts this fundamental superiority of the masculine principle as axiomatic:

> These two the first and last proportions are,
> The one imperfect, mortall, fœminine;
> The other immortall, perfect, masculine.

(*Faerie Queene*, ii. ix. 22)

then perhaps take it as rounding off the argument, and see the whole poem as based on the conception of male initiative, and of men and women as unequal partners in the creation of love: man the active, woman the passive, man's love the soul of their union and woman's the body.

I am prepared to put this forward as the most probable interpretation of this poem; but I do not do so with any firm conviction. With a great poem, its centre, its unity of moral tone or feeling, should be self-evident. But there are poems, and I think this is one, where there is an uncertainty as to the central conception which no amount of argument can settle with finality. There is a wobble in the line of thought in the second verse; and the last three lines are grammatically and metrically isolated in a way which suggests that they are making a special point. If we read the poem one way, the point seems a cheap one: if we read it the other, it does not seem sufficiently important to warrant its position as the poem's final statement. This is the kind of occasion on which biographical information could be of help. Here I cry out for some dates. If I could date this poem, and date Donne's other lyrics, I might be able to support one or other reading by reference to the poems which Donne was writing at about the same time. Or if I knew how old he was when he wrote it and whether he wrote it to any particular person, I might use this information to argue that this or that reading is the more likely in the circumstances in which the poem was written. Or, if we had Donne's notebooks and could see from drafts how he had begun and worked at the poem, we might find a clue. If we saw how the poem began we might feel more certainty about the intention of the poet. For it is the poet's intention which is not clear in the poem. For that reason I have to decide that it is not a wholly successful poem. The amount of ink that has been spent on its twenty-eight lines suggests that it has had at any rate many unsuccessful readers, of whom I am one.

I take this poem because my sense of failure with it tells me what I mean by success as a critic: the recognition of the poem's intention, which leaves me free to enjoy the poem. If this is to be guilty of 'the intentionalist heresy' I am quite content to be excommunicated for it. A poem is not whatever I choose to make of it. It is something which its author made with deliberation, choosing that it should say this and not that. Whether he made it with ease, so that it 'came right', or with great labour, rejecting this phrase, or altering that, changing his plan in mid-stream, enlarging the scope of the work, or contracting it, he made it, as far as he was able, to his own satisfaction, recognizing, when it was finished: 'This is what I meant to say.' He may not have known all that he meant to say when he began; but some conception, either clearly formed before he began to write, or growing as he wrote, governed his creation, so that the final poem had unity of thought, feeling, rhythm, and diction. The power to recognize this conception, which is the source of the poem's life in all its parts, and to read the poem in its light, is what I mean by true judgement in a critic.

The Limits of Literary Criticism
(RIDDELL MEMORIAL LECTURES 1956)

I

THE DRUNKENNESS OF NOAH

Writing in *Lux Mundi* in 1889, in the famous essay on 'The Holy Spirit and Inspiration', which provoked such a storm, Charles Gore declared: 'A literary criticism is being developed, which is as really new an intellectual product as the scientific development and, as such, certain to reverse a good many of the literary judgements of previous ages.' When I was honoured by the invitation to deliver these lectures, I thought that the best way I could fulfil the intentions of the foundation[1] was by a discussion of modern methods of literary criticism and of the problems they raise; since literary criticism has an obvious bearing on a matter which is of great importance to Christians, the interpretation of Holy Scripture. Gore was stating in his generation, with his characteristic prophetic insight, what is stated afresh in every generation, and always as if it were a new discovery, that the Bible, whatever else it may be, is certainly literature, and presents to the human understanding literary problems, and demands that we exercise upon it the methods and skills appropriate to the discussion of such problems.

When Gore spoke of a new literary criticism he had in mind

[1] The terms of the Deed of Foundation demand that the lectures should be concerned with the relation between religion and contemporary developments of thought, 'with particular emphasis on and reference to the bearing of such developments on the Ethics and Tenets of Christianity'.

developments in that literary criticism of the Bible which
came into being in the nineteenth century and distinguished
itself from textual criticism under the name of Higher Criticism. But his words can be given a wider extension. Since he
wrote, the study of literatures ancient and modern has become
an autonomous study in universities, and literary criticism has
become conscious of its scope and methods as a distinct intellectual activity. It has become a professional study. I would
not wish to suggest that the remarkable developments which
have taken place in the literary criticism of the Bible in the last
hundred years are a result of the practice of literary criticism
in our schools of English literature in the universities. It
would be futile to attempt to establish priorities between the
New Testament critic and the Shakespearian critic, each finding old answers insufficient, and attempting to frame new
questions which will give better answers. But that there are
connexions, some arising from the intellectual habits of the
age, some due to a process of cross-fertilization, is obvious to
anyone reading recent studies in the two fields. As a professional student of secular literature, I tend to feel when I read
certain recent works of New Testament criticism that I am
finding familiar tools taken up and used on unfamiliar material.
I do not doubt that the New Testament scholar reading some
recent studies of Shakespeare's plays might feel the same sense
of being at home and not at home. It is anyhow undeniable
that a writer who asserts today that a problem in the New
Testament is a literary problem and requires a literary solution
means something very different from what Jowett, or Matthew
Arnold, or Dean Farrar, or even Charles Gore would have
meant by such a statement. Developments in literary criticism

and the problems they raise are therefore of concern to those who hold the Christian faith, and I thought that some such conception of the relevance of my professional studies might have been in the minds of those who so kindly invited me to give these lectures. At the same time, when I decided to draw some parallels and make some comments on fields so far apart as the criticism of seventeenth-century literature and the criticism of the New Testament, I realized that I was committing myself to saying perhaps little that was worthwhile on either. I am aware also that I may, in the one field through lack of detailed discussion, and in the other by sheer ignorance, appear to misrepresent the work of those more learned than myself. I can only hope that an attempt to show some connexions and to suggest some misgivings may be of interest to those in either field who are not aware of what is happening in the other, and may also have some bearing on the general problem of the purpose and the limits of literary criticism.

The literary critic is often spoken of as exercising one of two functions, interpretation or evaluation. Good criticism is said to enlarge and purify our understanding of a work, or to enable us to judge of its excellence. The division is an artificial one since neither function can be exercised without the other. Although the stress of a particular critic, or the nature of the particular work he is dealing with, may weight his criticism towards one or other of these ends, no judgement of a work's excellence is possible without understanding, and understanding is itself the fruit of an initial act of judgement seeking confirmation. Nobody wastes time interpreting what is not thought worth interpretation. It would, however, be generally true to say that the main stress of criticism in the last thirty years has been on the duty of interpretation, and that the major triumphs, and one might add the main aberrations, of modern literary criticism have been not in the region of judgement, but in the region of interpretation. This is in itself a sign of an evaluating judgement: the immense importance attached to literature, and particularly to poetry, in this century. Because imaginative literature has come to be thought of as one of the prime vehicles of knowledge, we see so many persons devoting their intellectual powers to the interpretation and detailed exegesis of poetry. Serious works of literary criticism have something of the same kind of place in publishers' lists today which sermons held for the Victorians. A feature of criticism is the treatment of poetry as if it were scripture. As a corollary, the literary problems of the New Testament are discussed in the terms in which poetry is discussed, and we have recently been asked to consider St. Mark, or whoever wrote the second Gospel, as having written what is from the literary point of view, 'more of a poem than a treatise'. The growth of the conception of the literary critic as primarily an interpreter, and changes in the conception of what is demanded of an interpreter of the literature of the past, have brought about the opposite of what it was thought would be the result of the injunction to read the Bible as we read any other book.

Thirty years before Gore, Benjamin Jowett contributed to *Essays and Reviews* in 1859 an essay on 'The Interpretation of Scripture', which also provoked a great storm. Jowett had none of Gore's sense of the disturbing possibilities of literary criticism. The concept of reading the Bible as we would read any other book was to him a simple and simplifying one. It meant brushing aside the accretions of time and the dust of theological controversy, and going back to the true meaning of Scripture, 'the meaning which it had to the mind of the prophet or evangelist who first uttered or wrote, to the hearers or readers who first received it'. It was, of course, necessary to understand the historical circumstances, be aware of the presence of outworn modes of thought, and analyse the peculiarities of the writers' language; but Jowett plainly assumed that these were not difficult tasks, and that it was a relatively simple matter to recognize the meaning words had for those who uttered them in an alien language two thousand or more years ago. The test by which the true meaning could be recognized was an apparently simple one: 'The universal truth easily breaks through the accidents of time and place.' For Jowett believed that 'the world changes, but the human heart remains the same'. As we read Jowett's essay an image arises in the mind of how he envisaged the events behind the Gospel records. He conceived them in terms of what he held dearest and holiest. A teacher is speaking to a group of serious, but not highly educated, working-men, attempting to inculcate in them a loftier and sweeter morality. This is to him the core of the Gospels, their true meaning. When he turned to the Old Testament, as a book made up of many books, he saw in it a record of the history of an ancient people whose religious customs and moral conceptions culminated in the high ethical monotheism of the prophets. The plain sense and true meaning of the Scriptures is for Jowett historical. Although the writers' own historical sense was faulty, we can, by the exercise of critical judgement, glean from them a record of the growth of mankind's sense of the holy and the good.

The conception of progress makes us able to derive profit from all the books of the Bible. We can discern in all what speaks to the best in ourselves, stripping off the husks and finding the kernel of moral and religious truth. It did not seem to strike Jowett that he was invoking the historical sense in order to be able to ignore it. The writers of the Old Testament were not concerned to furnish materials for nineteenth-century historians, and the writers of the New Testament presumably related miracles because they thought them of significance. Jowett looked for 'the meaning which Scripture had for those who first uttered it' in order to be able in some measure to discount it.

If we pass from Jowett to Arnold we are passing from the world of critical scholarship to the world of higher journalism. In *Literature and Dogma* in 1873 Arnold declared, again as if it were a fresh discovery, that the Bible was a book and must be read as we read other books. His master-keys to the interpretation of Scripture were 'a fair mind' and 'the tact which letters, surely, alone can give':

> For the thing turns upon understanding the manner in which men have thought, their way of using words, and what they mean by them. And by knowing letters, by becoming conversant with the best that has been thought and said in the world, we become acquainted not only with the history, but also with the scope and powers, of the instruments which men employ in thinking and speaking.

It is well known what Arnold, approaching the Gospels with a fair mind and literary tact, found there. He found in their central figure a 'new and different way of putting things', 'what is indicated by the expression *epieikeia* or "sweet reasonableness" '. He declared that we could leave out all matters which he called 'theosophy', since Jesus himself preferred to describe himself by the simplest term 'Son of Man', and that we could leave out all matters about the Church, because 'Jesus never troubled himself with what are called Church matters at all; his attention was fixed solely upon the individual.' These remarks no doubt appeared grotesque to anyone acquainted with serious biblical criticism in Arnold's own day. They are grotesque to us as a piece of literary criticism, even if we have only a rudimentary acquaintance with New Testament problems. It seems fantastic that anyone sitting down today to read the Gospels with a fair mind and literary tact should think 'sweet reasonableness' the dominant note of the Lord's teaching. He would be much more likely to emphasize the dark sayings and to point to the uncompromising nature of the demands made upon the Lord's disciples. But, further, Arnold's whole approach seems to us unliterary. He has not asked any of the questions we should ask and seems unaware of the kind of question which interests us. He is not, on the one hand, attempting to make sense of a single work, one of the Gospels. Nor is he asking in what circumstances or for what purpose these works were written, or what the words and phrases the writers employed meant to them. The lack of interest in particular works as self-subsistent objects, to be apprehended as wholes, and the lack of interest in the historical circumstances in which a work came into existence, are consequences of Arnold's general theory of literary criticism. He was interested in trying to sum up writers by some expressive formula which would epitomize what he found most valuable in them, and was not interested in the elucidation of a work as in some sense independent of all its writer's other works, an aesthetic whole, or in analysing the idiosyncrasies of a writer's modes of thought and expression in the context of the thought of his age, the two main preoccupations of literary criticism today. The lighthearted manner in which Arnold approaches the problems of the interpretation of Scripture is a consequence of the fact that he did not consider elucidation and interpretation to be tasks to engage the higher faculties. These were shown in the appreciation of what was of lasting value in the work. Arnold's literary tact responded to the moral fervour of Hebrew literature, its passion for righteousness. This was its abiding significance to which the literary critic should point. Behind the Gospels he felt the moral renewal which Christianity brought to the ancient world, and saw Jesus of Nazareth as a greater and gentler prophet.

Arnold's criticism is the criticism of a man of letters. To Charles Gore, writing in 1889, literary criticism was a more serious and professional affair. It was primarily analytical. It meant distinguishing the different strata in works whose single authorship had been taken for granted, the study of sources, the recognition of literary forms. By its light the historical books of the Old Testament could be shown to be idealized and interpreted history, and other books, which appeared superficially to be historical, could be shown to be quasi-dramatic compositions put into the mouths of historical persons; while the earliest records of the Jewish race were to be treated as myths and legends, sometimes semi-allegorical. This strictly limited definition of literary criticism, which makes it anterior and ancillary to interpretation and evaluation proper, was the orthodox meaning of the term in biblical studies still in 1928, when it was defined very clearly in an essay by E. J. Bicknell in the *Commentary on Holy Scripture* edited by Gore and others for the S.P.C.K.:

Literary criticism investigates the date and authorship of a writing, the circumstances under which it was composed, the scope and purpose and nature of the work. It asks such questions as whether it is the production of one author or more than one; whether it is based on or embodies earlier writings; and if so, what is their date and character, and have they been altered by the editor.

I think, even as late as 1928, many teachers of literature in the universities would have defined literary scholarship in much the same way, and distinguished it from the criticism of men of letters.

Gore's essay belongs to a different world of discourse from Jowett's, because his whole discussion of the interpretation of Scripture is set in the context of a profound consideration of the doctrine of the Holy Spirit and the nature of inspiration. But he agrees with Jowett and Arnold in one thing: he emphasizes, as they do, that the historical sense is the primary sense of Scripture and he dismisses the mystical sense as wholly uncongenial to the modern mind. Nearly forty years later, in his preliminary essay in the S.P.C.K. *Commentary* in 1928, he put forward essentially the same view:

Thus we heave a sigh of relief when we discover that the great St. Thomas lays it quite decisively down, basing himself on St. Augustine, that no argument on behalf of the faith is to be based on any allegorical interpretation of Scripture. And he adds that we lose nothing scriptural thereby 'because nothing necessary to faith is contained under the spiritual sense of Scripture, which Scripture does not somewhere deliver manifestly through the literal sense'.

But by 1928 matters had changed so much that, in spite of the editor's statement, there was included in the *Commentary* a long essay by Dr. Darwell Stone on the mystical interpretation of the Old Testament, with a plea for its recognition as of high spiritual value and the statement that in his judgement 'the Church is not likely to be able to retain the reading of the Old Testament and the recitation of the psalter in public worship unless the use of the mystical interpretation is to some extent recognized'. A note to this essay was appended by Dr. Charles Harris, a specialist in the Wisdom literature, calling for 'a fresh treatment of mystical interpretation which shall distinguish between its arbitrary and its rational use'.

To Jowett, all attempts to look for a hidden meaning in Scripture were ludicrous: 'That the present age has grown out of the mystical methods of the early fathers', he wrote, 'is a part of its intellectual state. No one will now seek to find hidden meanings in the scarlet thread of Rahab, or the number of Abraham's followers.' But he went on to point out that, although his readers might smile at the excesses of the early Fathers, 'who have read the Bible crosswise, or deciphered it as a book of symbols', remains of the method survived 'whenever there is departure from the plain and obvious meaning', adding severely: 'If words have more than one meaning, they may have any meaning.'

Jowett's disciple and admirer Dean Farrar, who supplied Jowett's demand for a history of the interpretation of Scripture in his Bampton Lectures of 1885, which he dedicated to Jowett, supported Jowett's position with a splendid range of what he regarded as wholly preposterous interpretations. His learned and entertaining book is a mine of information. It is

written in a highly tendentious, vigorous manner, well sea-
soned with epigrams. He put forward, as Jowett did, the basic
axiom that 'all Exegesis must be unsound which is not based
on the literal, grammatical, historical, contextual sense of the
sacred writers. . . . It is impossible that we should rightly
apprehend the meaning of that Book otherwise than by
linguistic and literary laws.' The mystical interpretation of
Scripture was to Farrar a source of endless exasperation. How
could intelligent men be so wrong-headed? He summed up
the work of the Alexandrian Fathers by saying: 'They do but
systematize the art of misinterpretation. They have furnished
volumes of baseless application without shedding upon the
significance of Scripture one ray of genuine light.' The *Liber
Formularum Spiritalis Intelligentiae* of Eucherius, the first
writer to distinguish the anagogical sense as implying reference to the heavenly Jerusalem, he dismissed as 'a dull and
desultory dictionary of metaphors'. He paid a noble tribute to
the great Origen as founder of all Christian biblical study, the
father of its textual criticism, and of grammatical as well as
allegorical exegesis; but over Origen, the exegete of the spiritual senses, he could only shake his head with despair: 'Arbitrary in its purport, immeasurable in its extent, a great part of
this allegoric comment becomes a mere shuffling of subjective
commonplaces.' Such comments 'do but weary and offend us
with a sense of incongruous unreality. They change tender
human narratives into dreary and ill-constructed riddles.'

I am aware that in quoting Jowett and Farrar I am citing
Liberal Churchmen and that a different and tenderer attitude
towards the comments of the Fathers would be found among
the High Churchmen; but it was pre-eminently the Liberals

who demanded that the Bible should be interpreted in accordance with literary laws. There is some irony in the fact that the
literary criticism which they so confidently invoked to establish a single plain sense of Scripture has, by its own development, led men away from a historical interpretation of the
Bible to a theological one. Further, the method of seeking for
the spiritual sense, so far from seeming an incomprehensible
aberration of the human intellect, has become not merely
comprehensible but extremely sympathetic. The sleep of
Adam, the ark of Noah, the passage of the Red Sea, the thread
of Rahab, and even, 'most shocking of all' as Farrar calls it,
the drunkenness of Noah, interest the literary student, as well
as the student of Scripture, much less as human narratives,
tender, exciting, or grotesque, than as significant in something
of the same way as they were to the early Christian centuries.
They are read as symbolic stories which have meaning beyond
their value as narratives, and call for interpretation in some
'spiritual sense', as myths or symbols embodying some kind
of inner truth.

The mystical interpretation of the story of Noah drunk and
naked in his tent,[1] which so deeply shocked Dean Farrar,

[1] And the sons of Noah, that went forth of the ark, were Shem, and Ham,
and Japheth: and Ham is the father of Canaan. These are the three sons of
Noah: and of them was the whole earth overspread. And Noah began to be an
husbandman, and he planted a vineyard: and he drank of the wine, and was
drunken; and he was uncovered within his tent. And Ham, the father of
Canaan, saw the nakedness of his father, and told his two brethren without. And
Shem and Japheth took a garment, and laid it upon both their shoulders, and
went backward, and covered the nakedness of their father; and their faces were
backward, and they saw not their father's nakedness. And Noah awoke from
his wine, and knew what his younger son had done unto him. And he said,
'Cursed be Canaan, a servant of servants shall he be unto his brethren.' And he
said, 'Blessed be the Lord God of Shem; and Canaan shall be his servant.'

happens to provide an admirable example of this change of attitude. Many visitors to Venice must have been struck by the choice of this episode from the Old Testament as the subject of the sculpture on one of the three beautiful corner pillars of the Doge's Palace. The first pillar, next to St. Mark's, shows the Judgement of Solomon. Its appropriateness is obvious outside the seat of government and palace of justice. The next, on the corner facing the lagoon and Piazzetta, shows Adam and Eve plucking the apple, with the tree between them. Again, it is highly appropriate that the first sin and the beginning of human history should be represented here. On the opposite corner, however, instead of the expected parallel to the Tree of the Fall, is to be found the figure of Noah drunk. He is shown leaning upright against the vine-tree which he had planted, with his two good sons turning away from the sight of his nakedness and holding a robe with which to cover his shame. In the mosaics of the atrium of St. Mark's, as culmination of the story of Noah and the ark, there appears again this episode of Noah drunk. This time Ham is shown, mocking his father's nakedness and calling to his brethren. In two even more famous works of art this same episode is prominent. It occupies the foreground of the panel devoted to the story of Noah on Ghiberti's gates for the Baptistery at Florence, and it is the final episode of Michelangelo's series on the roof of the Sistine Chapel at Rome. But on Ghiberti's gates and on Michelangelo's ceiling Noah lies prostrate, whereas on the Doge's Palace he is standing. The reason for this difference is clear if one looks at the whole design. In the panel immediately above that portraying the story of Noah, and in the same corner of the panel as the corner below in which

Noah lies drunk, Ghiberti placed the creation of Adam, with Adam prostrate, being raised from the ground by his Creator. Similarly, on the roof of the Sistine Chapel it is the figure of the newly created Adam rising from the earth which parallels the prone figure of Noah drunk. In each series Noah is set over against Adam, as type of the second Adam who is Christ. On the pillars of the Doge's Palace the reference to the Passion is more obvious, because the pose of Noah leaning against the vine reminds the spectator of a Deposition or Descent from the Cross. The reference to the Passion in the recumbent Noah is not in the same way suggested to the eye.

This manner of thinking appeared little short of blasphemous to Dean Farrar, and indeed most persons without literary training, whether Catholic or Protestant, whom I have asked whether they could see any connexion between the Drunkenness of Noah and the Passion of Christ have shared Dean Farrar's sense of irreligious absurdity at the suggestion of a connexion. But most literary persons, though few have been able to explain precisely how Noah here typifies Christ, have not felt this sense of absurdity and impropriety, and have been willing to entertain in their minds the notion that this queer old story in Genesis has a meaning, and that the reason it was preserved in Genesis was that it had some meaning, although the meaning the writer intended may not necessarily be its true meaning.

The story was early referred to the Passion by Cyprian, who equated the wine Noah drank with the cup of the Passion. But the fully developed mystical interpretation, which we find in the *Glossa Ordinaria*, and which lies behind the very frequent representation of the episode in art, was given by Augustine in his *Contra Faustum*. It owed its existence to the well-known principle that anything unedifying in Scripture should be interpreted in a spiritual sense, and to a second principle, that a figure who typified Christ in one thing, as Noah saviour of the human race did, must typify him somehow in everything related about him. Noah, having planted a vine and drunk the wine of it, was drunken and naked in his tent. What else can this signify, asks Augustine, but that Christ drank of the cup of the Passion and suffered death among his own people the Jews—*in tabernaculo suo*? His nakedness is the mortality of the flesh—the death which was a scandal to the Jews and to the Gentiles foolishness, but to 'them that are called both Jew and Greek', that is to Shem and Japheth, the power and wisdom of God. Ham the mocker is unbelief. The sons who will not look upon their father naked, and look only upon the robe with which he will be covered, are those who did not consent to the death of Christ and will look upon it only through the veil of the Sacrament. Over against Adam and Eve and the Forbidden Tree, the Doge's Palace shows Noah leaning against his vine and the two sons holding up the veil. They typify the new creation in Christ. On Ghiberti's doors and on Michelangelo's ceiling the remaking of mankind through the death and resurrection of Christ is symbolized by the parallel between the recumbent Adam and the recumbent Noah: 'For as in Adam all die, even so in Christ shall all be made alive.'

Such an interpretation of the old story does not seem strange to those who are familiar with the work of art-historians, and who have made their pilgrimages around

French cathedrals under the guidance of M. Emile Mâle, or to the literary student familiar with the hidden senses of Scripture from the work of scholars on *Piers Plowman*, and from recent popular studies of Dante. But it is not merely a wider dissemination of historical knowledge, a kind of antiquarianism, which has made scriptural symbolism congenial once more. This particular story struck the imagination of Simone Weil. She was apparently unaware of the standard interpretation from Augustine and of the popularity of the subject in late medieval art. She fastened upon it as embodying a truth about ancient civilizations and interpreted it mystically for herself. She was, in fact, doing just what Augustine had done, extending the typical sense; for she knew, and claimed as justification for her reading, that Origen had said that Noah was Christ. Out of her intense repugnance for Jewish exclusiveness she evolved her own interpretation of the story's true meaning. The Jews, who preserved the story, falsified its significance, because they made Ham accursed for looking on his father's shame and praised the sons who refused to look and covered their father's nakedness. But the truth of the story, she declares, lies in the fact that the Jews alone of Mediterranean people forbade wine to their priests, and rejected the mystery religions in which men looked upon the death of God. The Egyptians, in their mysteries, contemplated the death and dismemberment of Osiris, and they taught the Greeks, the sons of Japheth. Only the Semites remained obstinately blind. When the time of fulfilment came, the sons of Shem rejected the revelation of Christ's Cross. To Simone Weil, Noah was known to the Egyptians as Osiris, and to the Greeks as Dionysus: all are types of Christ. In this ancient story is shadowed the mystery of the God who speaks in weakness and in nakedness, and dies and is dishonoured; who is not the God of power, the Lord of Hosts, who is worshipped by the children of Shem. The sons who would not look were refusing the knowledge of the Cross.[1]

Simone Weil is declaring that the true meaning is quite other than the meaning the original writer intended. The writer in Genesis plainly told the story to justify the triumph of the Israelites over the Canaanites. Ham is the father of Canaan who is cursed and devoted to bondage, while Shem is blessed and exalted over him. The Christian Fathers saw its true meaning as a prophecy of Christ, in accordance with their conception that the whole of sacred history was the revelation of God's actions towards men which culminated in the creation of the new Israel by the new Covenant. They were, to some degree, developing the original meaning, or at least the spiritual sense they found did not wholly contradict the literal. They were giving a new content to two fundamental Jewish ideas: the Jewish sense of the otherness of God, whose name must not be uttered, and whose Face no man can see and live, and the fundamental Jewish conception of election and calling, of some being chosen and blessed and others being rejected. Simone Weil brushes the literal sense wholly aside, and finds the true meaning in terms of her own deepest conviction: that God speaks in secret to all men and that the Christ who was rejected by the Jews was known to the pagans. Because of this fundamental belief she does not, of course, limit herself to seeing types of Christ in Scripture. She can

[1] See Simone Weil, *Attente de Dieu* (Paris, 1950), pp. 177–89; see also *Lettre à un religieux* (Paris, 1951), pp. 43–45.

write of a passage from Sophocles which she has been translating: 'The interpretation which sees Electra as the human soul and Orestes as Christ is almost as certain for me as if I had written these verses myself.'

I quote this as an extreme example of a habit of mind of our age which shows itself in many ways, the looking for a hidden or true meaning. The method of 'mystical interpretation' can hardly any longer be said to be 'alien and repellent to the modern mind'. On the contrary it is plainly only too fascinating. The work of anthropologists studying primitive myths and rituals supports it, as does the work of psycho-analysts analysing dreams by the interpretation of symbols. The efforts of philosophers constructing theories of symbolism, the discussion of the language of poetry as a symbolic language, and the conception that the work of art is a symbol, objectifying experiences which defy conceptual expression, have encouraged critics of literature to look below the surface of narratives or dramatic actions, and the thread of the discourse of a lyric, in an attempt to discover the realities which the writer is symbolizing, and find personal symbols or archetypal myths. Some critics have found it convenient to make use of the old terms of scriptural interpretation and have spoken of literal, moral, and mystical senses. I found the terms useful myself when I was trying to suggest that the subject of Mr. Eliot's *Four Quartets* could be regarded in various ways. I was, perhaps illicitly, using the terms in quite another way from the way their original inventors used them, and so, I fear, adding to intellectual confusion. But it has been explicitly declared that the old method of four-fold interpretation needs 'refurbishing' and bringing up to date, in order 'to make partially available to reason that complex of human problems which are embedded deep and imponderable in the Myth'.[1]

The growth of this habit of mind has coincided with a marked tendency in literary studies which, at first sight, would seem to lead towards very different results in the field of interpretative criticism. In field after field theories of composite authorship, earlier versions, different strata have been discarded. The kind of analysis which was once thought to be the particular duty of literary criticism is now markedly out of fashion. The assumption today is more and more in favour of single authorship, unless there is clear external evidence to the contrary, and of taking works as they stand and not postulating earlier versions to account for inconsistencies. Even where the inconsistencies in the work as published are as glaring as they are in *The Faerie Queene*, most people would agree with Professor C. S. Lewis that it is 'quite impossible to reconstruct historically the phases in Spenser's invention of which particular inconsistencies are, so to speak, the fossils', and would applaud him for taking the poem as it exists and not speculating on its growth. This general movement in scholarship has gone on side by side with the rise of the so-called 'ontological school' of criticism, whose main axiom has been the necessity of interpreting a work by itself. 'Make sense of what you have' has been the motto with both scholars and critics, if I may for the moment accept what is an unhappy distinction. The importance of the single author and the single work dominates literary studies, as can be seen if the plan and treatment of the new Oxford History of English

---

[1] William Troy, quoted by R. S. Crane, *The Languages of Criticism and the Structure of Poetry* (Toronto, 1953), p. 114.

Literature, now in progress, is compared with that of the old Cambridge History. 'Schools and influences' are out of fashion. Old disintegrating theories which assumed that Shakespeare spent much of his career revising other men's plays, and later attempts to show him as almost continuously engaged in revising his own, theories of *Beowulf* being based on heroic lays, and later theories of a pre-Christian *Beowulf* were all in the air, or at least being debated, thirty years ago, although they were then being increasingly challenged. The modern undergraduate is not troubled with these discussions. Occam's razor has been applied to the critical postulates beloved by nineteenth-century scholars. The modern scholar or critic concentrates in the first place on making what he can of his text as it has come down to him. There has been a strong reaction against the study of even extant and known sources, much more against the discussion of hypothetical ones. Why should we trouble ourselves with the source on which a poet worked, it is asked: what matters is what he has made of his material, not where he quarried his stone, or what was the shape of the unsightly lumps before his chisel transformed them into a significant masterpiece.

I hope it will not be thought that I am implying that all this is merely our fashion. The gains in knowledge which this concentration upon the object itself has brought are solid and unquestionable. Literary criticism and scholarship have rightly learned from the sciences the importance of isolating problems, of defining the scope of an investigation, of not multiplying hypotheses, and of starting from what is known. But it is interesting that so many scholars working independently and in widely different fields have felt the hypothesis of single authorship to be the obvious and fruitful one, whereas to our grandfathers it was the opposite hypothesis which they assumed to be the more probable and the one more likely to prove fruitful in results.

Trends in literary scholarship thus give support to critics who regard it as their duty to see works as integrated wholes, and the body of an author's work as a totality proceeding from a single mind. Many critics would say that their prime task is to display the individuality and particularity of a work or of an author: to lay bare the inner principle of its organization, if their study is of a single work, or the modes of operation of a writer's imagination, if the study is of a writer's works generally. The methods employed are the close analysis of the language, and particularly the study of the images, considered as symbols whose recurrent use creates patterns of meaning, through which we apprehend the real content of the work or the prime and dominant concerns of the writer.

At first sight it would seem that critics of this type who are concerned with what is called 'structure', defined by an influential critic of this school as 'a pattern of resolutions and balances and harmonizations, developed through a temporal scheme', would come to very different conclusions from the critics referred to earlier who look in poems and plays for dominant themes or underlying archetypal myths: that a critic who insisted on the individuality and uniqueness of a work of art would differ greatly from a critic who insisted that poetry was myth or vision. But although there are marked differences between critics who are mainly concerned with 'tension', the inner coherence of the poem, and critics whose concern is with themes, which have recently been explored very acutely by Professor Crane, I do not feel that anyone acquainted with the range of modern interpretative criticism is as much aware of these differences between them as of what the two schools have in common. Whether the critic is looking for what lies behind the images or for a meaning which is created by their interplay makes in practice very little difference to the reader's impression. He feels in either case that he is being confronted with what he might unphilosophically describe as a distinction between what the work says and what it means.

Origen himself reported that critics of his methods of scriptural interpretation complained: 'Hoc divinare magis est quam explanare.' Explanation, or making plain, is not a word much used in critical circles today. An older word has been revived, and 'explication', or the process of unfolding or bringing out what is implicitly contained in a work, is the term favoured by the interpretative critic. He has become a solver of riddles.

II

THE POETRY OF ST. MARK

I⊤ would not, I think, have been possible for a Christian before this generation to use such a phrase as the 'poetry of St. Mark'. If the word poetry implies the use of all the resources of verbal expression, obviously St. Mark was not writing poetry. Most of us, who are virtually Greekless and accustomed to the language of the Authorized Version, find it difficult to realize what an obstacle the style of the Gospels presented to cultured men of the first Christian centuries. It was one of those affronts which Christianity constantly affords to fastidiousness. The Old Testament was a different matter, much of that could be regarded as poetry of a high kind, and Isaiah could be praised by the scholarly Jerome as a 'man well-born, of urban speech, with no taint of rusticity'; but to the educated convert of the first centuries the Gospels were the writings of uneducated men, using a debased literary instrument. They had 'no form nor comeliness'. This would seem to have been particularly true of the Gospel of St. Mark, and it has been suggested that its comparative neglect in the early centuries may be explained by its suffering in comparison with the more literary and sophisticated Gospel of St. Matthew. Even in the Authorized Version the second Gospel is conspicuously lacking in verbal attractiveness. We do not go there if we wish to illustrate the subtle, haunting beauty of the rhythms of our Bible. On the contrary, as soon as criticism had established its priority, St. Mark's Gospel was valued precisely because of its lack of literary quality. Its unevenness, roughness, and abruptness made it precious. The author was described as giving the impression of being 'a faithful "interpreter" of another man's ideas, unversed in literary artifice, Greek in speech, but a native Jew in all that lies behind speech', and was regarded as having provided 'the most direct and literal transcript for posterity' of the life of the Lord. When it is declared that St. Mark has written something nearer a poem than a treatise, it is not meant that St. Mark is a lord of language, a literary artist. A person who speaks of the poetry of St. Mark is not making the same extension of the meaning of the word as we make when we speak of the poetry of, for instance, Sir Thomas Browne.

On the other hand, a person using this phrase is not offering any opinion as to how far the events described by the evangelist actually occurred, or how far they occurred as he described them. No contrast is necessarily implied by this phrase between poetry and history. The poetry of St. Mark does not mean the fiction of St. Mark. The contrast between a poem and a treatise is a contrast between one manner of discourse and another: between language used to express an imaginative apprehension, whether of events, persons, or experiences, and language used for logical discourse and argument, or to give information. By the time we have read through the Gospel of St. Mark nothing has been proved, and we have not acquired a stock of verifiable information of which we can make practical use. In that sense reading the Gospel is like reading a poem. It is an imaginative experience. It presents us with a sequence of events and sayings which combine to create in our minds a single complex and powerful symbol, a pattern of meaning. Reading St. Mark is quite unlike reading a series of entries made by a compiler of annals, or a collection of separate anecdotes. The growth of the conception of poetry as essentially symbolization has made it possible for someone to speak of the 'poetry' of St. Mark; as it has made it possible for a writer to discuss a work of profound historical scholarship such as Gibbon's *Decline and Fall* and a romantic prose fiction such as Sidney's *Arcadia* under the same term as 'epics'. St. Mark is called a 'poet' because he was not concerned to narrate mere events, but to narrate meaningful events which compose a meaningful whole.

To Jowett and the exponents of the Liberal school of theology the Gospels were materials out of which it was hoped that historical criticism and analysis might be able to construct a biography. I suppose Dean Farrar's *Life of Christ* is one of the best popular monuments of that endeavour, a work containing a great deal of historical and topographical information. The school of literary critics to whom Gore was referring, the source critics, occupied itself with literary analysis of the documents in their relation to each other. It was inspired by the methods and skills of textual criticism, from which the so-called Higher Criticism developed, which always seeks to reduce the number of witnesses. Its great triumph was the establishment of the priority of St. Mark, a result which one imagines will never be questioned. It found itself obliged to postulate a second primary document to explain the relationship of St. Mark to St. Matthew and St. Luke. This 'Q' hypothesis was generally agreed to have solved the Synoptic problem, and left the Fourth Gospel standing apart as the 'theological Gospel'. Very recently, in accordance with the tendency which I have referred to, which has been operating in the discussion of such problems, the necessity of postulating 'Q' has been challenged. I am not competent to judge the merits of the argument and do not know how it has been received. I am only interested in the method and the assumptions which the questioner works with. The doctrine that we should make all we can of our extant documents before we make hypotheses about lost earlier ones has always been honoured in theory in these matters. It is applied more and more strictly because a different view of 'making sense of what we have' prevails. In this case it rests on the assumption that we must take seriously the imaginations of the writers of the Gospels ascribed to St. Matthew and St. Luke. It may seem rather old-fashioned to refer to the writers of the Gospels under their traditional names, with the title of saint; but in fact this is not so. One of the results of the new literary approach to the Gospels is that it has restored the traditional conception of four distinct writers to whom we must give personal names. Whether the names are historic or literary names is another matter; but they are names that mean persons through whose imaginations our own imaginations are illuminated.

The triumphs of source-criticism raised problems which could not be solved by its methods. If St. Mark's was the earliest Gospel, its date appeared to be between the years A.D. 65 and 70, nearly forty years after the events which it purported to relate. The pressing question then became the form or forms in which the material the writer was using came to him, the manner in which the traditions were preserved. Form-criticism, which originated in Germany at the opening of this century, set itself to answer this question, not from guesses about what happened in the early Church, but from a rigorous analysis of the Gospels as they stood, which aimed at separating out materials of different kinds. It broke the narratives up into little sections, which could be compared with each other and whose form could be analysed; studied the links between the sections; and considered reasons for grouping certain stories together. The methods of form-criticism revealed that whether or not there was a chronological reason for the grouping of certain stories, there was certainly a topical one and this could be demonstrated. The fundamental question which the form-critic asks is 'Why was the story told?', or 'What is the point of the story?' The form-critic assumes that the meaning or point of the story has preserved it and has shaped the form in which it is told, so that what the story means and the way it is told are inseparable. The stories are seen as apologetic or dogmatic in intention. This method of treating the Gospel stories is very different from the method generally current before, by which the story was first elaborated and expanded by historical and geographical detail, a certain amount of psychological surmise was indulged in to make the narrative dramatically vivid and human, and it was then asked what could be learned from the story. This, which was the classic method of meditation on the life of Christ, was to a great extent also the method of scholarly interpretation. The form-critic does not consider the story and then look for the meaning; nor does he attempt to expand or fill out the laconic narrative. The shape of the story has been

dictated by the significance and through this shape the significance can be understood. The story is not to be expanded, but
interpreted as it stands. The form-critics distinguish two distinct types of narrative, the literary story, told with a certain
amount of artistic elaboration, and the concise story, where
only the bare elements of an episode are given. Within these
large divisions they distinguish certain narrative patterns,
such as various kinds of miracle stories, and 'pronounce-
ment' stories, whose point is that they lead to a significant
saying.

The emphasis of the form-critic is on what is called 'the
Gospel behind the gospels', or the Apostolic Preaching, or
the *Kerygma*. Its exponents display the Gospels as the expression of the mind of the teaching Church. Dr. Lightfoot judged
the great merit of this school of criticism to be its emphasis
'on the vital connexion between the little sections, including
the teaching, of the gospels and the great fundamental, permanent Gospel themes of vocation, physical and spiritual
restoration, life and death, love and hate, judgement and
salvation'. He went on to say: 'It was probably to the light
thrown by the historical traditions on these great themes,
even more than to their historical interest, that the traditions
themselves owed their preservation; and if form-criticism can
show once more the vital connexion between the gospels and
the Gospel, it will have proved its value.'[1] In the hands of its
extremer exponents form-criticism can seem to reduce the
Gospels to collections of sermon-anecdotes, composed, and
some, it is implied, invented, to make a dogmatic point. In
the hands of a master who combines power of critical analysis

[1] R. H. Lightfoot, *The Gospel Message of St. Mark* (1950).

with a delicate literary sense it can be most rewarding, as in a recent essay by Professor Dodd in which he applied its methods to the narratives of the appearances of the Risen Christ.

In their emphasis on 'themes', the English critics, who have employed and profited by the methods of form-criticism, have shown the same preoccupations which have been dominant in the criticism of literature. Behind the little story or section lies the *significatio*, or rather the significance is not so much behind the story as within it: it has preserved the story and shaped it. And the significance is primarily apologetic or theological. The Church produced its 'gospels as the expression of its Gospel'. Dr. Lightfoot's discriminating use of the capital is itself a highly significant symbol. The little stories are recorded because they are symbolical of the truth and the actualities of our salvation, whether or not they represent the truth and the actualities of historical occurrence. This is why they have been preserved in the form in which they have come down to us. It is their 'meaning' which matters, because it was for this that they were told.

All the same, form-criticism, particularly in its extremer manifestations, is not congenial to the temper of mind which regards it as the first duty of the critic to make sense of literary wholes. It disintegrates the separate Gospels, and is open to the literary objection that it is not dealing with the work itself, but with the materials out of which it was made; and these materials, the oral preaching of the Apostles, do not exist; they are irrecoverable except by deductions from what we have. It can be complained that the form-critic has reduced St. Mark to a mere piecer-and-stitcher-together of materials already given form by others. The questions which form-criticism raises but cannot by its own methods and on its own assumptions answer, in its search for 'the Gospel behind the gospels', are 'Why was a Gospel produced?' 'What is a Gospel, considered as a literary form?' or 'What kind of model, if any, had St. Mark in mind when he sat down to begin to write the first Gospel?' He can hardly have thought of himself as setting out to write a memoir. Memoirs are not a Jewish form; and, anyhow, his work has no resemblance to a memoir, as a glance at its opening words will show. The newer method of criticism of the Gospels is both a development from, and a reaction against, what one of its foremost exponents, Dr. Austin Farrer, has described as the attempt 'to shoulder St. Mark out of the way and lay our hands on his materials'.

I do not know whether Dr. Lightfoot, whose *History and Interpretation in the Gospels* and *Locality and Doctrine in the Gospels* are singled out by Dr. Farrer as 'two classics of the new method', was aware of how closely in its search for a symbolic or theological pattern in St. Mark's Gospel, his work paralleled the interpretative work of many literary critics, particularly the critics of Shakespeare. With Dr. Farrer there can be no doubt. He approaches the literary criticism of the New Testament with a mind steeped in secular literature both ancient and modern, and he shows himself fully aware of the parallels between what he is doing and what is being done by modern critics of poetry. How whole-heartedly he has adopted the methods of modern literary criticism can be seen from his handling in *The Glass of Vision*, the Bampton Lectures for 1948, of a classic problem in the New Testament. He took there as an example of a problem which demands a literary solution the abruptness with which St. Mark's Gospel breaks off at the eighth verse of the sixteenth chapter, with the flight of the women from the empty tomb and the words 'for they were afraid': ἐφοβοῦντο γάρ.[1]

Dr. Farrer declares that the question whether St. Mark can have intended to end at this point is essentially a literary question, and that if we are to defend this abrupt ending as the intended ending of the work we must do so by literary arguments. Gore would have agreed; but he would have been much startled by the kind of arguments employed. We must, if we are to defend the abrupt ending, 'try to persuade ourselves that we have been missing the true poetic pattern of the book':

Either, like some of Mr. Eliot, it defeats us at first sight, through our failure to pick up the crucial literary allusions; or we have been reading it through a haze of memories of St. Matthew and St. Luke, and not in its own clear light. The purpose of our arguments must be to show that the last line is inevitable in its finality—we must show that, so far from its being impossible for St. Mark to stop here, it would be impossible for him to go on.

Dr. Farrer undertakes to show this by considering theme, recurrences of phrase, and sequences of narrative, and by noting the occurrence of images with underlying symbolic reference. He points first to what he calls the theme of the entire Gospel. 'The act of God always overthrows human expectation: the Cross defeats our hope; the Resurrection terrifies our despair.' Throughout the passion narrative, he

[1] It is generally accepted that the last twelve verses, or 'Longer Ending', Mark xvi. 9–20, and the 'Shorter Ending', two sentences found in some manuscripts, were neither of them written by the author of the Gospel.

declares, this is the dominant idea. Men do not know what to do with the divine when it is in their hands. A woman anoints the Lord's body for glory, and is told she has done it for his burial; the apostles attempt heroics, but at the crisis they flee; priests condemn him to preserve their priesthood which is to be destroyed; Joseph buries him whom no sepulchre can hold; women bring spices to embalm the already risen God: 'The mere rustling of the hem of his risen glory, the voice of the boy in the white robe, turns them to headlong flight.' Such an analysis reminds the literary student of many similar treatments of poems, designed to bring out the 'irony' and 'paradox' which a notable school of modern critics think the essential differentiating quality of poetic speech.

Dr. Farrer then turns to argue from grounds of phrase, recurrent rhythms, and 'formal recurrences of St. Mark's poetical magic', examining two parallel sections: 'one describing the last experiences of Jesus in the body at the hands of his disciples, the other describing the body of Jesus in the hands of his disciples after his death'. The first begins with the woman's anointing him at supper, followed by the giving of the sacramental body and the promise: 'I will go to Galilee.' In a garden a watch is set, but at the crisis all forsake him and flee, among them a youth in a linen cloth, who left it in the pursuers' hands. In sequence two, Joseph of Arimathea obtains the body and wraps it in a linen cloth: three women bring perfumes to embalm it. Entering they see a youth in a white stole. He bids them tell the disciples that Jesus goes before them into Galilee. Dr. Farrer then draws out the parallels between these sequences to show how they display the 'theme' of 'human perversity', and so comes to the linen winding-sheet, the boy in linen, and the boy in the white robe. 'There is surely some symbolic motif here', he says, 'if we could only hit upon it.' He begins by reference to Jewish customs. The priestly watchers in the Temple who were caught sleeping on duty had their robes taken from them. The young man's loss of his garment is a dramatic symbol of the idea 'Caught asleep on duty'. The sleeping guard was stripped of his robe of honour and had to slink away naked of glory. The naked body of the crucified is wrapped in fine linen to bestow honour upon it. But when the women come to embalm the body, it has been clothed in the radiance of glory, which the white stole of the angel by the tomb signifies. Lastly there is the name Joseph. Why has the name of this minor figure in the story been preserved? The man from Arimathea is a true Joseph when he begs the body of Christ from Pilate, as Joseph the patriarch had gone to Pharaoh to beg him that he might give his father Jacob burial in the land of Canaan. And at once, when we see this, other echoes of the story of Joseph can be heard. The boy who fled away leaving the linen cloth in his pursuers' hands recalls Joseph fleeing from Potiphar's wife, leaving his garment behind. Most of all, Joseph was betrayed by his eleven false brethren, buried in prison, and believed dead. But, in due course, he appeared to the brethren who had betrayed him as one alive from the dead, clothed in a robe of glory, as the man of the king's right hand. But when he said to them 'I am Joseph', his brethren could not answer him 'for they were confounded': ἐφοβοῦντο γάρ. The last words of St. Mark's Gospel echo the very words of the Septuagint, when Joseph thought dead revealed himself to the eleven who had sold him.

'St. Mark's words', comments Dr. Farrer, 'are shaped by a play of images and allusions of the subtle and elusive kind which belongs to imagination rather than to rational construction.' It will be noted where the images come from. The Christian Fathers were concerned to defend the ancient Scriptures as the revelation of the one God and Father of the Lord Jesus against Marcion and the Gnostics. For this reason they looked everywhere in the Old Testament for types and figures of the New, to bind together the two Covenants. Today the process is in a sense inverted, in that it is the New Testament which is being interpreted through the Old. A literary criticism which sees narratives as organizations of symbolic images sees everywhere in the New Testament the images of the Scriptures on which the writers' imaginations had been nourished from childhood. How else should these writers express their belief that the God of Israel had indeed visited and redeemed his people except through images coloured by the memory of the images of his great deliverances of old?

The methods of literary criticism and analysis which Dr. Farrer was applying here he employed on an extended scale in his *A Study of St. Mark* in 1951, and developed them further, with considerable modifications of earlier discussions and conclusions, in *St. Matthew and St. Mark* in 1953.[1] They

[1] In this latter book he reopened the question of the ending of St. Mark's Gospel and put forward rather different arguments from those I have summarized from *The Glass of Vision*. He also modified his first account of St. Mark's 'cyclic imagination' when he came to treat St. Mark with St. Matthew. In a volume in memory of Dr. Lightfoot, *Studies in the Gospels*, edited by D. Nineham (1955), there are various essays applying these methods to other problems. Dr. Farrer's essay 'On Dispensing with Q' can be found here; and also Dr. Dodd's application of the form-critical method to the narratives of the appearances of the Risen Christ. It is only fair to say that in the chapter

bring together what have sometimes been regarded as conflicting canons of interpretation: the canon that it is the work itself which the critic is concerned with, and the canon that interpretation must take into account the writer's intellectual milieu. As well as finding pattern and significance by analysis of the work as it stands, Dr. Farrer is guided by something else. He is not content to assert, as some of the more reckless interpretative critics do: 'This meaning is there, because I have demonstrated its presence. Whether the author intended it or not is something we can never know. He is not here to be cross-examined, and if he were he might well refuse to add to what he has written; as many persecuted modern poets do, who, when asked what their poems mean, reply that they mean what anyone can make of them.' A conception of how St. Mark, a Greek-speaking Jew of the first century, would have thought is present, as well as a conception of how the human mind operates. The object of the inquiry is how St. Mark thinks. We are to arrive at a meaning which he would have recognized as what he meant.

By this method, the Gospel, considered as a work of literature, is seen as a great effort of symbolization, which we shall apprehend as we concentrate upon the lesser symbols which it integrates into its total pattern, until we see them all cohering into a structure of meaning. St. Mark, when we read him thus, is seen to have no need to give us narratives of the Risen Lord's appearances to the disciples. His whole Gospel is a great and complex symbol of the Resurrection, faith in which

referred to in the Bampton Lectures Dr. Farrer was only demonstrating the *kind* of arguments which should be employed in discussing whether a work has a proper conclusion. Later, he argues that a final concluding sentence has been lost.

is its pre-supposition. This is the Gospel informing his Gospel. By the time we have read to the end, with minds alert to the recurrent patterns, the rhythms of thought, the cycles in which his mind expressed itself, this 'Gospel' will have become an apprehensible reality to us. We must be aware too of the whole word of Old Testament images and symbols with which his mind is stored and of the habits of mind natural to a man of his time and race. He was accustomed to search the Scriptures, to think of the Hope of Israel as figured forth in great figures of the past: Moses the saviour of his people, Elijah the prophet of the Most High, David the anointed king. Those words 'Son of Man' which were to Arnold so touchingly simple and human in their appeal, so wholly free from 'theosophy', meant something very different and much more complex to a writer steeped in the Book of Daniel and the later Jewish Apocalypses. A new historical approach, as well as a different attitude to poetry, has made it impossible to regard the notion of Scripture having hidden senses as an aberration of the Alexandrian Fathers. The New Testament came into being in a world which was everywhere accustomed to look for esoteric meanings. The Scriptures had been allegorized, as the works of the pagan poets had been allegorized before them. It was a world in which numbers, colours, and jewels were pregnant with symbolic meanings. The Scriptures which St. Mark was brought up on had come to him loaded with interpretation and comment.

Dean Farrar thought of the Christian expositors as inheriting a fatal legacy of Palestinian and Alexandrian interpretation from the Rabbis and Philo, and stigmatized them for their 'wholesale intrusion of the subjective into the field of revelation'. He treated the New Testament writers as if they were largely isolated from this infection, on a small island of their own, lifted above the seas of nonsense that raged beneath and around. The historical approach to literature in his day meant the study of the political, social, and economic conditions under which writers worked. Today it means pre-eminently the attempt to take into account, and, more ambitiously, to recover, older ways of thought, and to learn the assumptions and presumptions out of which men wrote. The attempt to re-create the 'climate of opinion', sometimes rather inappropriately called 'background' of a period, is a distinctively modern enterprise. If anyone had used the phrase 'the world of the New Testament' fifty years ago, he would have been expected to be referring to the conditions in Palestine under the Roman occupation. Today the chances are that a book bearing this title would be concerned with belief in the power of demons, concepts about the destiny of Israel, and eschatology.

The best way, perhaps, to sum up the revolution which has taken place in the last thirty years is to quote from the S.P.C.K. *Commentary* of 1928 the note on the admittedly puzzling episode of the young man who fled away leaving behind the linen cloth:

The *certain young man* has of late been generally identified with Mark himself; in which case the introduction of the episode, otherwise meaningless, would be at once accounted for—Mark wanted to bring in his own solitary point of contact with the Gospel story. The details given suggest that the lad had got out of bed in his night-clothes to follow our Lord and the Twelve to Gethsemane: it looks as if he belonged to the house where the Last Supper had been held, was perhaps aroused by the chanting of the final psalm, and then with a lad's adventurous curiosity had determined to see things to the end. If he was a son of the house, his father was well acquainted with our Lord and so he may have heard talk about the danger to which the Prophet of Galilee was exposed, and the animus of the Jewish authorities against Him, after His dramatic cleansing of the Temple: a lad's enthusiasm may have re-inforced a lad's curiosity, and when the Apostles all fled he still 'followed with him'. When we remember further that Mark's mother Mary had a house in Jerusalem large enough for many Christians to meet in, and central enough for Peter to turn his steps to after his deliverance from prison, it must be admitted that, though the elements of this reconstruction are conjectural, they connect astonishingly well together.

To return to this after reading Dr. Farrer is like returning to Bradley after a course of reading in modern studies of symbolic patterns in Shakespeare's plays. A parallel development could be shown in discussions of such problems as the unexplained appearance of a third murderer in *Macbeth*.

I am not competent to discuss these methods of criticism in the field of the New Testament. I have neither the linguistic, nor the historical knowledge. My concern with these questions is that of a Christian whose profession is the study of English literature. I am in something of the position of an historian, or doctor, or barrister, or clergyman, who has always loved poetry and read it for pleasure, and who has bought, let us say, a recently published volume called *Interpretations*, a collection of articles on 'How to read a Poem', or has been listening to a series on the Third Programme called 'Reading a Poem'. As a professional student of literature I should be interested to hear his views. But I cannot presume to think that my views are likely to be of equivalent interest to a New Testament scholar, for the amount of specialized information and technical competence required in the two fields is not comparable. All the same I hope it may not be thought wholly absurd for me to make some general comments before turning to a discussion of the application of these methods in fields where I have more knowledge.

Dr. Farrer, with his accustomed clarity, puts a main difficulty when he says that some readers may have felt that under Dr. Lightfoot's guidance they were 'rediscovering the evangelist and losing the facts of the evangel'. This difficulty Dr. Farrer addresses himself to answer. He believes, as any Christian must, that 'the principal importance of St. Mark's Gospel lies in its historical content, and a main object of any study in the pattern and movement of the evangelist's imagination must be to assess more accurately the bearing of his historical testimony'. St. Mark's imagination has shaped his apprehension of events into a certain expository pattern, because his imagination apprehended a meaning in those events. If we can follow the movement of St. Mark's imagination as he develops the theme of his Gospel, understand, for instance, the symbolic significance of his thirteen miracles of individual healings, his two feedings of the multitude, and see how each section repeats, yet expands, and unfolds itself in the next, we shall see that the expository pattern is derived from a fundamental conception. This fundamental conception is the idea of prefiguration, which is the evangelist's mode of historical thinking. Once we grasp this we are in a position to consider St. Mark as an historian, and can translate the history he is relating into our own untheological pattern of history, which looks for causes and effects. By understanding how St. Mark understood history, we can arrive at a narrative sequence which is in our sense of the word historical. This leaves St. Mark with a philosophy of history and us with a bleak little summary of events.

But my difficulty does not lie here. I am dissatisfied because this method does nothing to illuminate, and indeed evaporates, St. Mark's sense of what we mean by historical reality, the 'Here and Now' of our daily experience, the 'Then and There' of memory, by which I do not mean detailed precision of testimony, but the deep sense of 'happening'. Surely a literary criticism of the Gospels must take into account this quality, which has struck, and strikes, reader after reader. I have in mind here, as a contrast to the method of interpretation through patterns of symbolic images, a remarkable piece of literary criticism which illuminates precisely this: the chapters in which Professor Auerbach in his *Mimesis, or the Representation of Reality in Western Literature* discusses the story of the sacrifice of Isaac in Genesis and the episode of Peter's denial in the Gospel of St. Mark. He compares Homer with the Old Testament writer to demonstrate the difference between legend treated as poetry and the sacred legend of the Jews, whose historical reality the writer believed in. After his discussion of St. Mark's narrative, he declares that he can find nothing comparable in any antique historian for sense of actuality.

The second difficulty I feel arises from distrust of an assumption which underlies much interpretation in terms of the 'ways of thought' of an age. It seems often to be taken for granted that because something is present and obvious in one place it must be assumed to be present, although it is not obvious, in

another: that because writers of this age were plainly habit-
uated to allegorical interpretations and thought frequently
in terms of types and figures, we can assume they never
thought in any other way. The presence of so much deliberate
and explicit reference to the Old Testament in the New casts
some suspicion on the notion that the writers would, in any
matter where it was important, be content to leave the reference indirect. They were not, after all, we must assume,
attempting to be indirect, allusive, and subtle. St. Paul thought
it proper to explain clearly his little allegory of the two sons
of Abraham, adding 'which things are an allegory'; and the
writer of the first Epistle of St. Peter again thought it necessary to state precisely that the Ark was a 'figure' of baptism.
I find it hard, therefore, to believe that the first readers of St.
Mark would have been as ingenious in picking up symbolic
references as is suggested. Further, it is agreed that St.
Matthew is often concerned to clarify and expand what St.
Mark has left enigmatic. If, as Dr. Farrer has argued, there
is a deep and important significance in the numbers fed, the
numbers of loaves, and the numbers of baskets of fragments
left over, it is difficult to see why St. Matthew, repeating
the conversation in the boat after the Feeding of the Four
Thousand, contented himself with explaining the relatively
simple metaphor of the 'leaven of the Scribes and Pharisees'
and made no attempt to explicate the riddle of the numbers.
Number symbolism, like statistics, is notoriously susceptible
of varying interpretations. I cannot believe the significance of
these numbers, if they have symbolic significance, was so
luminously clear to the first readers of the Gospels as is
suggested by St. Matthew's failure to clarify St. Mark's

'riddle'. Or are we to assume that St. Matthew himself did not see the point nor any other commentator before the twentieth century?

It may be that I am confusing an attempt to discover the writer's intention with an attempt to discover the way 'his mind works', although I am not quite sure in reading studies such as this that their authors are not hunting both hares at once. I am aware that the notion that we can grasp, and having grasped, should respect, a writer's intention has been much scoffed at; but if a writer's intention is difficult to come by, which is not in my view in most cases true, the 'way his mind works' is far more of a will-o'-the-wisp. When a writer's first drafts, scraps of memoranda, and 'doodles' have been preserved, we may possibly have a limited success in tracing the workings of the creative imagination, though even there the results are highly speculative. To attempt to do this backwards from the finished work is like weaving ropes of sand. I do not doubt that St. Mark's mind, like all human minds, was something of a rag-bag of memories, in which ideas and images and phrases jostled together and got 'hooked together' by processes of association. It may be that the name Joseph brought to his mind the story of Joseph the patriarch and this dictated the actual words he used to describe the amazement of the women. If the reminiscence was unconscious, it does not very much concern us. Such verbal echoes are a trick of thought whose presence we are often aware of in talking to friends. An odd phrase will strike us and temporarily distract our attention from what is being said until, having hunted it down, we once more pay attention. If it is intended to suggest that St. Mark was modelling his narrative consciously on the story of Joseph, the notion cannot, I think, stand examination. The three suggested parallels, Joseph fleeing from Potiphar's wife, Joseph asking Pharaoh's leave to bury his father, and Joseph appearing to his brethren, are in the wrong narrative order. The motives of the flight of Joseph and the young man's flight are entirely different: Joseph was saving his honour, the young man losing his, if that is what the loss of the white garment signifies. And the main point of the narrative of Joseph's revelation of himself to his brethren is their ashamed recognition of him. Conscious literary influence does not work like this. The parallel between the Septuagint and the last words of the Gospel is purely verbal. It prevents us from thinking that the words are as odd a conclusion to a sentence as we might have thought. It does not make them any less queer as the end of a book. The relevance of the existence of any such reminiscences of the story of Joseph to what St. Mark was concerned to relate seems to me insignificant. The unhappy effect of much literary criticism of this kind is that, although undertaken with great seriousness and much intellectual energy, it leaves an impression of intellectual frivolity, as if the critic were concerned with anything and everything except what mattered to the writer and what matters to his readers.

I am quite certain that I have been in contact with the mind and imagination of Dr. Farrer. Since it is a lively and fertile mind and a profoundly poetic and Christian imagination I am grateful for the experience and for much matter for meditation. I have very little sense, after reading him, of having come nearer to the mind and imagination of St. Mark. This method of 'submitting ourselves to the movement of the writer's imagination', of discovering the pattern he has created through images and recurrent phrases, is perhaps again only another method of 'shouldering St. Mark out of the way'; this time to get at his 'imagination', which turns out to be a scheme, a way of thinking, which is curiously like what we are discovering everywhere. I am reminded of James Thurber's attempts to learn botany. He tried every adjustment of the microscope and with only one of them did he see anything 'but blackness or the familiar lacteal opacity':

And that time I saw, to my pleasure and amazement, a variegated constellation of flecks, specks and dots. These I hastily drew. The instructor, noting my activity, came back from an adjoining desk, a smile on his lips and his eyebrows high in hope. He looked at my cell drawing. 'What's that?' he demanded, with a hint of a squeal in his voice. 'That's what I saw,' I said. 'You didn't, you didn't, you didn't!' he screamed, losing control of his temper instantly, and he bent over and squinted into the microscope. His head snapped up. 'That's your eye!' he shouted. 'You've fixed the lens so that it reflects! You've drawn your eye!'[1]

If patterns are what we are interested in, and patterns are what we are looking for, patterns can certainly be found.

For all its apparent deference to history, in its reference to the history of ideas, the method is often oblivious of, and impatient with, the historical. Whoever wrote the Gospel of St. Mark was a man, not a disembodied imagination. He was writing a work in which his readers would find things able to make them 'wise unto salvation'. What differentiates his Gospel from all other messages of salvation, is the assertion that something has happened in the world of history. It is surely an

[1] *My Life and Hard Times*, ch. 8.

odd phrase to speak of St. Mark's imagination being 'controlled' by facts. If we believe that what he is recording *are* facts—and that is the crux of the matter between Christian and non-Christian—then it is surely filled by the wonder of those facts, and not merely respectful to them. It is curious that the study of images, which began from a high theory of the imagination's power to apprehend the truth and value of experience, and to express its apprehension of the world, has led only too often in practice to an ignoring of the primary imagination, which degrades the secondary, or creative, imagination into an instrument for perceiving analogies and making connexions.

No one's salvation [says Dr. Farrer] depends on the comparison between Joseph with his eleven false brethren and Jesus with his eleven cowardly disciples; or on the antique symbolism of the robe of honour; or on the inverted parallels which give opposite expression to the theme of human perversity. Do not let us suppose that these things are the substance of saving truth. The substance of the truth is in the great images which lie behind, in the figure of the Son of Man, in the ceremony of the sacramental body, in the bloody sacrifice of the Lamb, in the enthronement of the Lord's Anointed. What we have been looking at is a play of secondary images and ideas under the pressure of the great images.[1]

As I read this analysis of the 'play of images' which leads to the great images which lie behind, I murmur with Madame Sosostris, the famous clairvoyante of *The Waste Land*, as she sorts her Tarot pack: 'I do not find the Hanged Man.' The central image of a human life and death seems to have disappeared.

Reflecting on the course of his own life, Dr. Edwin Muir,

[1] *The Glass of Vision* (1948), p. 146.

whose poetry is particularly rich in mythological allusion and symbolic imagery, declared that he could not bring the meaning of his own experience into a neat pattern. When he originally published an account of the story of his life in 1940 he called it *The Story and the Fable*, making a division between the narrative of events and the inner life in which they were transformed into symbols. His emphasis in the title and in the book suggested that it was in the latter that the significance lay. When he republished the book in 1954 he was content to call it by the noncommittal title of *An Autobiography*, and his final summary of his life tells us why. In our memory certain events and persons, and certain events through which we have lived, stand out like boulders in a stream or great rocks among waves. This element of the 'given' in memory, resisting, and subsisting through, the transformations the mind makes, sharply distinguished from reverie and still more from dream, forbids the ascription of significance to fable over story. Significance appears to hover over their intersection. Of certain persons, and by analogy of certain events, we exclaim:

> Thou art so truth, that thoughts of thee suffice,
> To make dreams truths; and fables histories.

The same sense of historical reality, or otherness, inheres in works of art and cries out against the attempt to reduce their meaning to something which they symbolize. 'What is left to say when one has come to the end of writing about one's life?' asks Dr. Muir:

Some kind of development, I suppose, should be expected to emerge, but I am very doubtful of such things, for I cannot bring life into a neat pattern. If there is development in my life—and that seems an idle supposition—then it has been brought about more by things outside than by any conscious intention of my own. I was lucky to spend my first fourteen years in Orkney: I was unlucky to live afterwards in Glasgow as a Displaced Person. . . . Because a perambulating revivalist preacher came to Kirkwall when I was a boy, I underwent an equivocal religious conversion there; because I read Blatchford in Glasgow, I repeated the experience in another form, and found myself a Socialist. In my late twenties I came by chance under the influence of Nietzsche. In my early thirties I had the good fortune to meet my wife, and have had since the greater good fortune of sharing my life with her. In my middle thirties I became aware of immortality and realized that it gave me a truer knowledge of myself and my neighbours. Years later in St. Andrews I discovered that I had been a Christian without knowing it. I saw in Czechoslovakia a whole people lost by one of the cruel turns of history, and exiled from themselves in the heart of their own country. I discovered in Italy that Christ had walked on the earth, and also that things truly made preserve themselves through time in the first freshness of their nature.[1]

Living in Italy, and particularly in Rome, brought to Dr. Muir a profound imaginative experience, the experience of the significance of history, which came to a mind which had habitually thought of significance as to be sought primarily in myth. The primary historical imagination is that by which we know human beings and human experience and contemplate them and it seriously. If this is weak or scorned, attempts to understand how men once thought, and to re-create the past imaginatively, degenerate into mere antiquarianism on the one hand, and a reduction of individual human minds to schematic ways of thought on the other.

I cannot feel satisfied with a literary criticism which substitutes for the conception of the writer as 'a man speaking to

[1] Edwin Muir, *An Autobiography* (1954), p. 280.

men', the conception of the writer as an imagination weaving symbolic patterns to be teased out by the intellect, and in its concentration on the work by itself ends by finding significance in what the work suggests rather than in what it says, and directs our imaginations towards types and figures rather than towards their actualization. As literary criticism I cannot regard the new symbolical or typological approach to the Gospels as satisfactory. It does not explain a prime historic fact; that for centuries Christian emotion directed towards the historic person of Jesus Christ, true God and true Man, has found in the Gospels the strength of its own conviction that 'Christ walked on this earth'. I feel the same kind of dissatisfaction with the results of these methods applied to the interpretation of poetry. I am not happy at the assumption that there is a royal road by which we can get at 'meaning', and I am particularly suspicious when the critic buttresses the claim that he has found the 'meaning' with the statement that this was the meaning the work must have had for men of its own age, since we know how men of this age thought. To borrow the words of Dr. Muir, 'Things truly made preserve themselves through time in the first freshness of their nature.' It is the first responsibility of an interpreter that he should neither disregard nor damage that first freshness with which things made by long-dead men speak directly to the mind and heart.

III

THE HISTORICAL SENSE

THE first half of the seventeenth century is, perhaps, the period in which the method of seeking for meaning through the study of patterns of imagery and the axiom that we must attempt to think as men of a writer's age thought have been most generally and pertinaciously applied. Interpretation and explication, the discovery of underlying significances and profounder meanings, have claimed and received support from the obvious facts that allegorical writing persisted through the period, masques and pageants filled with allegorical and symbolic persons were popular, and there was delight in emblems and all kinds of insignia. It has also been asserted that men of this age, when they read what was to them the book of books, were still alert to the presence in it of hidden spiritual senses.

The audiences which watched the plays of Shakespeare and his successors, or at least the more serious members of them, were, we are told, accustomed to seeing the 'spirit in the letter' everywhere. Since the pattern of the old moral plays can be seen to correspond to the dramatic pattern created by the relations of Prince Hal to Falstaff and to the King, it may be assumed that the audience would recognize behind the drama of individuals an abiding conflict which they had often witnessed in simple moral form. They would thus be guarded against any sentimental sympathy with that grey-haired old Iniquity, Falstaff, who is a particular embodiment of the familiar figure of Riot misleading Youth. If we wish to understand the 'historical sense' of the play, that is the sense it had for the author who wrote it and the audience who first saw it, we must see its 'moral sense', and not allow ourselves to be seduced by any anachronistic sympathy for Falstaff. This particular application of the general theory has had a markedly debilitating effect on some recent productions of the first part of *Henry IV*, in which Falstaff has seemed so oppressed by awareness that he is temptation incarnate that he has had hardly the spirit to present any serious temptation.

As well as to moral senses it has been suggested that we should be alert to the presence of mystical ones, since typology was a familiar conception. Men were accustomed to seeing in Noah, the saviour of the remnant of mankind, or in Moses, the leader of Israel out of captivity, or in Joseph, the redeemer of the brethren who sold him, types and figures of Christ the Saviour of men. Would they not naturally then be aware, in watching dramas of human wills and passions, of a reflection, within the particular destinies shown, of the one great drama of human redemption? Thus we have been asked to see the mysteries of grace moving behind the human relation of Cordelia to the father who wronged her, and to recognize in the mysterious activities of the Duke in *Measure for Measure* an image of the Providence which while testing men brings good out of evil, and even in his marriage to Isabella the votaress a symbol of the mystic marriage of Christ and the soul. Prospero has long been allegorized as the poet, master of the creatures of his imagination. He appears more often now as a shadow of the Creator and divine stage-manager. The restorations to life, and recoveries of what was thought lost, in the last plays are discussed as images and symbols recalling those appearances in the flesh which apparently in its original form St. Mark's Gospel did not record.

The study of Shakespeare the poet, or of Shakespeare's imagination as revealed through the patterns of recurrent imagery in his plays, led at first either to the discovery of archetypal images, which related the plays to primitive myths and rituals, or to the discovery in them of symbols of the conflicts of the individual psyche in its attempts to come to terms with its environment. Critics who thus discovered myths, or archetypal images, or interpreted the plays in terms of Freudian psychology, were not, of course, unduly concerned if it was pointed out to them that their interpretation left out of account, or even conflicted with, important aspects of the play so interpreted. Thus Freud's interpretation of *King Lear*, as taken up by George Orwell, appears to ignore the moral feeling of the play by finding its truth in statements which Goneril and Regan would approve: they are great believers in the necessity of renunciation by the old. But interpreters of this kind are not claiming to be arriving at an 'historical sense'. Their concern is to get at something rather different: the source of the work's continuing power over men's imaginations, the truth of all time which lies within it. They treat the plays as Simone Weil treated the old story of Noah drunk; or, in Dr. Farrer's words, they study 'the play of the secondary images' in order to come at the great, perennially significant images which lie behind them. These great images vary according to the interpreter's own system of thought; but such interpretations usually end by resolving all the conflicts within a play into the conflict of various antinomies: 'Storm and Calm', or 'Light and Darkness', or 'Order and Chaos', or 'Death and Birth', or 'Youth and Age'.

Increasingly in recent years the great images have come to be images taken from the Christian myth of man's Fall and Restoration, and significance has been found in such concepts as Providence or Grace, and in a stress on the theological virtues. This is partly, I think, in reaction against the tendency of the great images to turn all too quickly into the great abstractions. To find the Garden of Eden behind a play is, at least, to find poetry behind poetry. Even more, it is because the more scholarly critics have been alarmed at the uncontrolled subjectivism of interpretation by patterns of images, and have wished to find external warrant for the search for patterns and confirmation of the patterns found. The habits of mind of the age have therefore been appealed to, particularly the persistence of the conception of the hidden senses of scripture, as a justification for the search for hidden meanings and as validating the meanings arrived at. More important is an obvious change in the general intellectual temper during the last two decades. There is a widespread recognition today, and this was by no means the case thirty years ago, that the story of man's Fall and his redemption through Christ is, at the very least, a myth of unique beauty and spiritual significance, and that the intellectual systems which have through the centuries been built into that story demand, at the very least, intellectual respect. It is by no means only Christians, who might be thought to have a special interest in claiming that the imagination of Shakespeare was a 'Christian imagination', who have come to these conclusions, and discovered through their study of Shakespeare the poet somebody not unlike Shakespeare the theologian.

As well as being used to justify symbolic interpretations of Shakespeare's plays, the habit of seeing the spirit in the letter is invoked to explain the superlative excellence of the poetry of the age of Shakespeare and the age of Milton. The loss of this habit is pointed to as one of the accompaniments, or even as a main cause, of an impoverishment of poetry in the age of Dryden and subsequently. Few people now hold in its rigour the extreme doctrine that the main stream of English poetry virtually dried up, except for a few trickles and isolated stand-ing-pools, between the decline of the metaphysicals and the appearance of the modern symbolist movement in the poetry of Yeats and Eliot. But many who would not subscribe to this view and would reject strongly the view which went with it, that Milton was a corrupter of the true English poetic tradi-tion, assert that something was lost in the mid-seventeenth century which we are learning, through the poets of our own day, and the efforts of the interpretative critics, to recover. It is argued that we must revive within ourselves the capacity to recognize hidden senses, and learn to read these hieroglyphs and forgotten symbols if we are to read the poets of this period with a full imaginative sympathy and be aware of the meanings which the author would have expected his readers to be sen-sible of and to respond to. He, like his readers, was a child of his age and we must learn its way of thought. Since a play or a poem is a structure of meaning conveyed through its images in their pattern, our first step towards making it meaningful to us is to be aware of the meaningfulness of the images to men of its own day. We can then, if the Christian images are not in themselves meaningful to us, see them as reflections of the great archetypal images of ancient myth.

Methods of literary criticism develop through dissatisfaction with older methods. The method of close analysis of the work through the study of its images developed from dissatisfaction with a criticism which seemed to be always discussing something other than the work: its sources, or the author's life, or social and political history as reflected in it, or whatever the work inspired the critic to muse about, whether human life in general or the previous or future history of the persons in a play. The combination of this method with a close reference to the climate of opinion or world picture of the age, as twin keys by which to arrive at a true meaning, arose from dissatisfaction at irresponsibility of interpretation and the fact that such conflicting interpretations were being arrived at. This method seems now to have come to the point where its deficiencies are becoming more obvious than its merits. The keys which have been cut and shaped with such care certainly open a door; but the door only seems to lead into another room with a door which is locked, and the lock on that door the keys do not fit. And the room we have got into is plainly not the heart of the building, but only another antechamber. Patterns have been found in plenty and meanings are being pointed to everywhere; but the true meaning of the work— its supreme value when we re-read it, or when we go to see it acted, or when the memory of it comes back to us—seems less illuminated than obscured by the interpreter's efforts. 'The true use of interpretation', said Jowett, 'is to get rid of interpretation, and leave us alone in the company of the author.'

It is impossible not to feel after reading much modern interpretative criticism that the author and his work have disappeared and that it is the interpreter's insistent company which we are left alone with.

The method has also led to odd results at which common sense revolts. The concentration on the working of the imagination in its power to perceive analogies and correspondences, and the allied concentration on the 'world picture' of the early seventeenth century, have led to the equation of things which are very different but which we are told we must regard as fundamentally the same. The desire of critics to examine the work as it stands, by a close study of its language and imagery, and the work of the historians of ideas, attempting to give the work an imaginative frame in the world picture of its day, have had the result of depriving particular works of their particularity, and of reducing the rich variety of one of the most richly various periods in our, or any other, literature to a kind of shadow play, hardly worthy the attention of the profounder critic who seeks for hidden meanings and underlying habits of mind.

Our own preoccupation with myth, metaphor, allegory, and symbol as related methods of expressing the imagination's sense of the unity of its experience has led to a concentration on the 'spiritual senses' of works which has made the literal sense something to be brushed aside as soon as possible. It is claimed that in so doing we are finding the true historical sense, since this was a continuing habit of mind which endured from the Middle Ages through the Renaissance into the seventeenth century and, to our impoverishment, was lost when at the close of the century the old 'medieval world picture' was replaced by the modern scientific one. This view, which is here stated in its crudest form, might be called, with no impoliteness intended, the myth behind much modern criticism of the poetry of the Elizabethan and Jacobean period. It embodies, as do all strongly held myths, some elements of truth; but it tells us more, I think, about those who framed it and hold it than about the sixteenth and seventeenth centuries, and reflects the preoccupations of the critic more than those of the author. It has led to the discovery of 'philosophical patterns' in Shakespeare's plays and the discovery of theological significances in the conduct of his plots and the shaping of his characters. It has led also to the equally surprising discovery that 'metaphysical wit and concord of unlikes in an image are precisely the operation much condensed of the old and (maligned) allegorical way of writing'; and to finding that the imaginative power of *The Temple* lies less in its 'picture of the many spiritual Conflicts that have passed betwixt God and my Soul', which Herbert, according to Walton, thought to be its main concern, than in Herbert's use of typology. In her epoch-making study of Spenser's *Faerie Queene* in 1934 Dr. Janet Spens insisted that we must not try to read Spenser as if he were Shakespeare, and that to treat his 'characters' as if they were characters in a play was to miss Spenser's whole significance. The opposite caveat seems called for today. It seems also necessary to reassert that metaphysical poetry is witty poetry, and condensation, although an element in all wit, will not alone give the effect of wit; and that Herbert's significance as a poet does not lie in what he shares with Quarles.

The unhistorical nature of this whole approach, in spite of

its insistence that we must not read our own ideas into the past, lies in its lack of interest in anything but ideas, its ignoring of events and circumstances, and its consequent reduction of individual writers, who are historical persons, to habits of mind, and of works of art, which are historical objects, to *exempla* of these habits of mind and repositories of ideas. For all its respect for the past it is, in fact, contemptuous of it. It substitutes for historical reality a kind of Golden Age of the Mind, when the difficulties which we feel as historical beings were not felt, when faith was easy, and man, knowing his place in an ordered system of things, happily saw correspondences everywhere, only slightly disturbed by the possibility that the universe might not be geo-centric. Four hundred years hence it might as well be said that men of the twentieth century were no longer haunted by the terrors that afflicted Johnson and men of his age, because the general acceptance of psycho-analytical theory, which the critic had demonstrated as present in work after work of literature, had, by providing an explanation of mental disturbances, shown the way to solve them. Whether we regard a past age as presenting us with awful warnings, or whether we regard it as giving us an example to be followed, and it is this latter and subtler form of patronage which the early seventeenth century has had on the whole to endure, we are emptying it of its own historical reality. It was to those who lived in it full of agonies, uncertainties, and conflicts and seemed, as every age does, a time of crisis, chance and change, as well as a time of confidence, advance and new knowledge. It was also, as are all ages, a time when everybody did not think alike.

Against this view that the power to see 'the spirit in the

letter' is the secret of the greatness of the greatest period in English literature, it would be equally possible—I think myself it would be truer—to claim that the growing sense from the twelfth century onwards of the importance of the letter and of the spiritual nourishment to be drawn from it was at the root of the greatness of much late medieval art, and that the insistence of Protestantism on the reading of the whole Bible, and on the primacy of the literal sense of the Scriptures is not unconnected with the flowering of our literature in the reign of Elizabeth. But I do not wish to set up one partial view against another and this is a subject too huge to embark on here. I would merely say that a study of how particular minds grappled with the problems of the interpretation of Scripture, bringing to bear on it what knowledge they had, is destructive of the notion that to men of this period, as Professor Willey has written, 'every statement in Scripture, whether narrative, psalm, prophecy, parable, vision or exhortation, had a "spiritual" meaning; that is to say, it was pointing, through its literal "sense", to a "Truth" beyond sense'.[1] My reading of the sermons and other prose works of Donne, and my attempts to follow him into the commentaries which he used, have brought me to the opposite conclusion.

Compared with other preachers of his Church and age, and certainly with those of the age preceding, Donne makes a great deal of reference to the mystical senses. It would be possible to amass a formidable number of quotations, and on their evidence argue, in all good faith, that Donne held the view which Professor Willey puts forward as the view of the age, and valued the mystical sense as the sweet kernel hidden

[1] Basil Willey, *The Seventeenth-Century Background* (1933), p. 60.

in the husk of the literal. Such a view, however impressively supported by quotation, would, I believe, be false. Donne's prime concern is always to establish the literal sense of his text, which he defines more than once as 'the principal intention of the Holy Ghost in that place'. He has profited by the long struggles of the exegetes of the Middle Ages to distinguish the problem presented to the interpreter of Scripture by its figurative nature, from the problem of whether it has different senses. Like St. Thomas, he includes in the literal sense the figurative, metaphorical, and parabolic. Thus he declares that in the first book of Scripture, Genesis, it is dangerous to depart from the letter, since we have no other means but this book to tell us how the world began; but in the last book, Revelation, 'there is danger in adhering too close to the letter':

The literall sense is always to be preserved; but the literall sense is not alwayes to be discerned: for the literall sense is not alwayes that, which the very Letter and Grammar of the place presents, as where it is literally said, *That Christ is a Vine*, and literally, *That his flesh is bread*, and literally, *That the new Jerusalem is thus situated, thus built, thus furnished*: But the literall sense of every place, is the principall intention of the Holy Ghost, in that place: And his principall intention in many places, is to expresse things by allegories; by figures; so that in many places of Scripture, a figurative sense is the literall sense.[1]

He is aware that in interpreting the figurative passages and expressions of Scripture different expositors have arrived at varying interpretations which he often spends some time in weighing. The test by which they are weighed and one preferred to another is 'the analogy of Scripture'. But what the

[1] *Sermons*, edited Potter and Simpson, vol. vi (1953), p. 62.

author primarily intended is always his first concern and very often he is content to rest there. His own interpreters might well take a hint from his comment on Pico's famous exegesis of the first words of Genesis:

> Since this was directly and onely purposed by *Moses*; to put him in a wine-presse, and squeeze out Philosophy and particular Christianitie, is a degree of that injustice, which all laws forbid, to torture a man, *sine indiciis aut sine probationibus*.[1]

In agreement with that statement of Aquinas which Gore read with a sigh of relief, that 'nothing necessary to faith is contained under the spiritual sense of Scripture, which Scripture does not somewhere deliver manifestly through the literal sense', he asserts again and again, in different ways: 'It is the Text that saves us':

> The interlineary glosses, and the marginal notes, and the *variae lectiones*, controversies and perplexities, undo us: the Will, the Testament of God, enriches us; the Schedules, the Codicils of men, begger us. . . . That book is not written in *Balthazars* character, in a *Mene, Tekel, Upharsim*, that we must call in Astrologers, and Caldeans, and Soothsayers, to interpret it.[2]

There is an interesting discussion in a sermon preached on Christmas Day 1621 on the text 'He was not that Light, but was sent to bear witness to that Light'. Donne considers the various uses of the word 'Light' in the prologue to St. John's Gospel. He objects to 'wresting in *divers* senses into a word, which needs but *one*, and is of it selfe cleare enough' and calls to witness other places in Scripture. He asserts that light is

---

[1] *Essays in Divinity*, edited Simpson (1951), p. 15.
[2] *XXVI Sermons* (1660), p. 47.

always used either in its natural sense, or, if figuratively, of God or Christ, and in no other ways. He therefore rejects the interpretation of some Fathers and of some of the 'Schooles' which would take 'Light' in the fourth verse as 'natural reason'. He sums up:

> Though it be ever lawfull, and often times very usefull, for the raising and exaltation of our devotion, and to present the plenty, and abundance of the *holy Ghost* in the *Scriptures* . . . to induce the *diverse senses* that the Scriptures doe admit, yet this may not be admitted, if there may be danger thereby, to neglect or weaken the *literall* sense it selfe. For there is no necessity of that *spirituall wantonnesse* of finding more than necessary senses; for, the more *lights* there are, the more *shadows* are also cast by those many lights . . . so when you have the *necessary sense*, that is the meaning of the holy Ghost in that place, you have senses enow, and not till then, though you have never so many, and never so delightfull.[1]

When Donne turns to what he calls in the *Essays in Divinity* 'the heart and inward Mine, the Mystick and refined sense', it is usually to the great classic types that he turns, primarily to the deliverance from Egypt, and also to the Psalms (whose Davidic authorship he, of course, assumes) as mystically interpreted of Christ. Even so, it is from David the historical King that he begins. 'All these things are literally spoken of David; By application of us; and by figure of Christ.' He made these three senses the basis of the plan of exposition for a set of six sermons on Psalm xxxviii, preached at Lincoln's Inn, and dated by his editors in 1618. They are early sermons. He does not usually in later life follow so rigid a plan. But it is notable that even here, where the plan of the

---

[1] *Fifty Sermons* (1649), p. 322.

sermon is based on the three senses, the exegesis of the literal sense and its application to us takes up far more space than the development of the mystical interpretation.

Donne's sermons provide more than one example of what can be described as interpretative literary criticism. An interesting one is provided by his discussion of a famous passage which had been interpreted allegorically by Philo and mystically by many Fathers, the appearance of three men to Abraham as he sat by the door of his tent in the plain of Mamre. The problem Donne considers is who were the three men. Were they 'three men, or three Angels, or two Angels and the third, to whom Abraham spoke, Christ, or was the appearance of these three a revelation of the Trinity?' First of all he distinguishes between Abraham's apprehension and Moses' relation. Moses said: 'The Lord appeared to Abraham', and therefore Moses intended us to understand that they were not ordinary men. But Moses also says that when Abraham lifted up his eyes he saw three *men*. We know that they were angels from the comment made on the episode in the Epistle to the Hebrews, but to Abraham they were simply men whom he entertained hospitably, and so he is here a pattern of hospitality to us. We too may 'entertain angels unawares' if we entertain strangers. On this point, following the Epistle to the Hebrews, Donne enlarges at great length. But was one of these angels Christ? This has been argued from Abraham's use of the term Lord, and his addressing the three in the singular. By comparison with other passages of the Scriptures Donne denies this and adds: 'When the Scriptures may be interpreted, and Gods actions well understood, by an ordinary way, it is never necessary, seldome safe to

induce an extraordinary.' God often proceeded with his servants by angels, it is not clear that he ever did so by his Son.
It is safer not to admit the notion here. So he comes to the last
question: whether, in these three messengers or angels, whom
Abraham addressed in the singular, we are to understand an
intimation to him of the Trinity. He turns to Luther, and
behind Luther to Augustine's *Figura nihil probat*, to which
Aquinas also had referred. There is no proof of the Trinity
here; but to those who believe there is a reminder of the
Trinity: 'It is an awakening of that former knowledge which
we had of the Trinity, to heare that our onely God thus mani-
fested himselfe to *Abraham* in three Persons.' He thinks the
Church of England right to appoint this as a lesson for Trinity
Sunday. We can legitimately 'exercise our own devotions'
with these 'similitudinary, and comparative reasons'.[1]

A study of how Donne handles this and similar passages in
Scripture has some bearing on our reading of Donne's poetry.
The clear distinction he draws between the literal and historical sense, the 'principall intention', which is fundamental, and
the similitudes and comparisons which we can, but need not,
use to exalt devotion and illuminate faith; the awareness of
the necessarily figurative and metaphorical nature of the
language of Scripture, which is included in the literal sense,
and of the 'secondary and dependent' nature of all 'allegorick
and typick' notions, throws a light on his use of similitudes
and comparisons in the conceit, which is not at all the same
thing as his use of metaphor. The essence of the conceit, and
the element which makes it witty, is that it appears to be arbitrary and a matter of intellectual choice. The poet appears to

[1] *LXXX Sermons* (1640), pp. 412–17.

be saying: 'Now I will show you what I mean, by a comparison or analogy. Take such and such a phenomenon for the
purposes of argument, and let me use it to show you what I
really mean.' Thus the similitude between parted lovers and
the separated feet of a compass is valued for its metaphorical
final statement of a personal relation:

> Thy firmness makes my circle just
> And makes me end where I begun.

And the fact that kings who put on taxes in time of war do
not remove them when peace comes leads to the beautiful
metaphorical statement:

> No winter shall abate the spring's increase.

Mr. Eliot spoke long ago of the blend of 'levity and seriousness' in metaphysical poetry. This remains a brilliant brief
description of its peculiar effect. We are avoiding its true
seriousness and finding seriousness in its levity, if we concentrate upon the imagination's power to perceive analogies and
neglect its primary power to apprehend and express what
touches the mind and heart. Where this is lacking metaphysical poetry is tedious trifling, or, to use the language of its own
age, the mere 'itch of wit'.

Typology similarly degenerates into a mere game, without
the sense of the actuality and importance of events and individual experience. It differed fundamentally from allegory in
having its roots in belief in the historical actuality of both the
type and its realization. Typologically, Paradise was not a
timeless Golden Age which might return again. It was a historical Garden, whose location could be discussed, in which
was figured the Church we enter at baptism, or the Heaven

which is the abode of the saints after death. The three terms were not reversible. Christ is not Moses or Elijah returned to earth: Moses and Elijah are not Christ. The conception of the irreversibility of historical events, or non-recurrence, which is behind the typology of the Old Testament, implies a doctrine of progress. There is a 'divine far-off event to which the whole creation moves'. New Testament typology differs radically from this in its assertion that the event has occurred, that the beginning and end of history are within history. This plainly modifies the Hebrew conception of progress and makes possible the fruitful if uneasy marriage between Hebrew historicism and Greek philosophy of which Christian theology is the child.[1]

When Philo allegorized the Old Testament to make its truths acceptable to the intelligent of his day, he was doing something different from what the Prophets of his race had done when they described the coming redemption of Israel in terms of the exodus from Egypt, the crossing of the Red Sea, and the entry into Canaan over Jordan. The Alexandrian Fathers, who followed Philo in finding moral allegories of the soul and the body, or of reason and the passions, everywhere, and who extended the typological or mystical sense to cover every text of Scripture, were departing from the Hebrew conception of history as the field of God's judgements and deliverances towards the other conception of history as a kind of pageant symbolic of eternal verities. Deeply attractive to the intellect and to some imaginations as this conception of the unreality of the particular is, it leaves unsatisfied the heart,

[1] For an attempt to distinguish true typology from its abuse, see J. Daniélou, *Sacramentum Futuri* (Paris, 1950).

which reflecting on its own experience knows that it has itself a history:

> But the heart makes reply:
> This is only what the eye
> From its tower on the turning field
> Sees and sees and cannot tell why,
> Quarterings on the turning shield,
> The great non-stop heraldic show.
> And the heart and mind know,
> What has been can never return,
> What is not will surely be
> In the changed unchanging reign,
> Else the Actor on the Tree
> Would loll at ease, miming pain,
> And counterfeit mortality.[1]

The Christian allegorizers went as far as they could to make tolerable to the educated of their day the sacred books of the Hebrews, which contained many episodes and many injunctions which seemed shocking to decency and to rational morality. The allegorical method, as has often been said, 'saved the Scriptures for the Church'; but the reason why the Scriptures had to be preserved was that it was believed that they contained the revelation of significant acts of God in history. This is, and always will be, the great stumbling-block to the Greek in us, the necessity of accepting an historical revelation.

For all its extravagances typology could never reduce its types wholly to symbols. Their symbolic value rested on their actuality. The tracing of continuing motifs in art is a fascinating study, but we must not forget when we follow Noah

[1] Edwin Muir, 'The Recurrence', *Collected Poems* (1952), p. 73.

drunk from Venice to Florence and to Rome, come home and find him in Salisbury Chapter House, and in the West window at York, and in the Holkham Picture Bible, as the type of Christ rejected by his own people, that there were other ways of regarding Noah which were current and which were just as valid. The Great Gloss contains a good deal more than the mystical sense which is what most people go to it for today. Here it records, under the name of Alcuin, a very rational excuse for Noah's lapse from sobriety. He did not realize that wine was intoxicating, suggests Alcuin, for there is no mention in the Bible of the cultivation of the vine before the Flood. Alcuin refers his readers to Jerome; it was also the comment of Chrysostom, the greatest of the doctors of the school of Antioch, which concentrated on the exegesis of the literal sense. I quote Alcuin because he is in the Gloss, and so has as good a right to be cited as representing a standard medieval view as Augustine. This conception of Noah as victim of his own inventiveness accounts for the presence of Noah drunk on Giotto's campanile, among other benefactors of the human race. He was the discoverer of the wine which makes man's heart glad.

In the sixteenth century Calvin and Luther took the same view of the episode which Donne takes when he quotes Noah's drunkenness and Lot's incest as examples of the fact that 'the vices and sins of great persons are not smothered by Scripture'. Bishop Hall speaks in the same way: he is distressed by Noah's lapse but excuses it on the ground that it only happened once. In case it should be thought that this is mere Protestant literalism, blind to the poetry of the Scriptures which Catholicism still responded to, I can call from the

Catholic side the Dutch Jesuit, Cornelius à Lapide, Donne's exact contemporary and the most voluminous commentator of the age. He refutes Luther and Calvin's severity towards Noah's inebriety, but not by turning from the literal sense of the story to a mystical sense. He merely quotes Chrysostom at them: Noah's lapse should not be regarded as sin, since it was due not to intemperance but to inexperience. Two and a half columns of his huge folio commentary on Genesis are given up to discussing this episode. They are almost wholly concerned with the historical sense and with references to the vice of drunkenness in antiquity and the Bible. At the close he comes to the tropological sense which he takes from Ambrose and Gregory. The story shows the impropriety of drawing attention to the misdemeanours of our spiritual parents, that is, ecclesiastics. In four lines at the close he just mentions the mystical sense from Augustine. I cannot think, in spite of its persistence in art, that the story of the drunkenness of Noah had very much spiritual significance to either Catholic or Protestant in the sixteenth and the seventeenth centuries, and no amount of illustrations in early Bibles will convince me to the contrary.

The mystical sense did not arise here from a sense that this was an historic turning-point in which the act of God could be seen, pointing to other greater acts to come. It arose from the desire to extend a type, in this case the Ark, and the desire to protect the moral reputation of the patriarchs. Both desires abated during the course of the Middle Ages.[1] But even if we

---

[1] See C. Spicq, *Esquisse d'une histoire de l'exégèse latine au Moyen Age*, Bibliothèque thomiste xxvi (Paris, 1944), and Beryl Smalley, *The Study of the Bible in the Middle Ages*, 2nd ed. (1952).

take the Ark itself as one of the fundamental figures in Christian typology, the type within the New Testament of our salvation by baptism, and recognize that the octagonal form of early baptisteries and fonts typifies the eight saved from the deluge, such conceptions are very remote from those deeply characteristic products of the later medieval imagination, the plays on Noah and his family. Obvious as this remark is, it is becoming necessary to insist that there are far more kinds of poetry in the Middle Ages than the poetry of Christian symbolism and courtly allegory. The imaginations of the writers of the Noah plays were just as much 'Christian imaginations' as was the imagination of the sculptor who carved the figurative Noah on the Doge's Palace. Their imaginations played over the literal and historical sense, seeing Noah as a man called by God to save the human race, a good craftsman, husband, and father. Looking at him in this way they were able to see him as comic, as well as holy and devout. Neither comedy nor tragedy can exist if the individual is only valued as illustrative of the general. It has been said that the Middle Ages lacked two essentials for a sound exegesis: 'une science philologique et surtout le sens historique'. But medieval literature and art testify everywhere to the response of the human imagination to historical reality.[1] There is continuity here, as well as in the survival of allegory. There is also a rich development.

In the field of seventeenth-century studies conceptions as to what was the 'climate of opinion' or 'world picture' have not provided an adequate check upon the essential subjectivity of

---

[1] This subject is handled at length by Erich Auerbach in *Mimesis*, translated Willard R. Trask (Princeton, 1953).

the search for meaning through the patterns of imagery. The conception of what the climate of an age was is equally at the mercy of a critic's own predilections. Just as patterns can be found when we look for them, so it is only too easy to build up, from a selection of current ideas and theories, schemes of thought, systems of ideas and, still more hazardous, habits of mind. It is inevitable and necessary that we should form such conceptions about historical periods, as we do about the temper of mind of our own times. We know from experience how such conceptions crumble when we talk with someone whom we had thought of as representing a particular modern attitude. Both a study of the patterns of images, and their part in the structure of a poem, and the knowledge of ideas, theories, and beliefs current in a period are of great value as tools in an interpreter's hands; but only if too much reliance is not placed on them. They cannot be more than auxiliary in leading us to the true 'meaning' of the work, which is the meaning which enlarges our own imaginative life. This is something we are aware of as present in the work before we attempt to analyse it, and as subsisting in the work after our analysis is made. The notion that this meaning can be arrived at by analysis is too ambitious. Literary criticism must begin by acknowledging its limitations. It can only give us approaches to the meaning, and an approach will be valuable in so far as the critic who employs it is aware of, and sensitive to, the value of other approaches. The analytic critic must be prepared to admit that description must often take over when analysis fails. All critics should acknowledge that the provision of information, analysis, and description can defeat the interpreter's true end, if he does not realize that, after a certain point, silence may well be the best service he can render his author and his reader.

One obvious defect of the concentration on the approach to meaning through form and pattern is blindness to the notion that meaning also inheres in style. It is not perhaps irrelevant to note here that there is some truth in the constant complaint that many distinguished, subtle, and perceptive modern critics themselves write with little personal distinction of style. The approach to meaning through form alone, the belief that 'in literature as in other arts meaning inheres in form' was commented on by D. H. Lawrence, writing of Thomas Mann, as 'the outcome not of artistic conscience, but of a certain attitude to life':

For Form is not a personal thing like style. It is impersonal like logic. . . . 'Nothing outside the definite line of the book' is a maxim. But can the human mind fix absolutely the definite line of a book, any more than it can fix absolutely any definite line of action for a living being?[1]

Lawrence was speaking of artists, not of critics, and comparing writers such as Mann, who 'has never given himself to anything but his art' with 'other artists, the more human, like Shakespeare and Goethe, who must give themselves to life as well as to art'. His comment can be applied equally to a critical concentration on what is called 'the logic of the imagination': it leaves too much out. One thing which it omits is style, which, although notoriously difficult to analyse, is a prime element in giving us a sense that particular writers and particular works have great value and meaning. It is one of the major

---

[1] *Selected Literary Criticism*, edited A. Beal (1955), p. 260.

elements differentiating a poem from a riddle, which once it has been guessed has no further power to interest.

There are a good many signs in recent literary criticism of a reaction against these methods, springing out of a truer historical sense than that which concerns itself exclusively with the history of ideas. Two recent studies illustrate this development very well. The writers have plainly absorbed the lessons to be learned from the critical approach which concentrates on works of art as self-subsistent wholes. Both take more seriously than some of the searchers for meaning have done the distinction between the use of the word 'symbol' to describe a work of art and its use in common parlance. They do not treat the works they discuss as reducible. While alert to the intellectual milieu of the works they are discussing, they see works of art as historical objects 'preserved through time in the first freshness of their nature' because they are the products not of 'ways of thinking' but of men.

In the first chapter of his Clark Lectures on Coleridge, delivered in 1952, Humphry House, whose early death is an irreparable loss, not only to his friends, but to literary scholarship, declared it was time to consider the dangers of discussing Coleridge as 'a mind', and said that by 'minimising the importance to Coleridge of the external world in which he lived, we run the risk of diverting attention from some of his most characteristic strengths as a writer'. He went on to defend the biographical approach, so long out of favour, and answered the commonplace that 'it is an impertinence to pity Coleridge' with a plea that we should show 'a proper pity' for great writers, the kind of pity which Aristotle was concerned to distinguish as appropriate to the contemplation of the tragic.

The justification of this human and compassionate approach to Coleridge and his writings can be seen later in the book: in the just, discriminating, and generous appraisement of the value of Robert Penn Warren's study of *The Ancient Mariner* in terms of themes and images, and the demonstration of how much this approach left unexplained and ignored. Nobody could imagine that Humphry House was advocating a return to the criticism of men of letters 'approaching the work with a fair mind and the tact which letters alone can give', or was suggesting that first impressions are all that matters. At the same time the historical nature of his approach is shown by the fact that it does not ignore, or depreciate that first apprehension of the work's meaning. Mr. Warren arrived at something so different from what a fascinated child finds on first reading *The Ancient Mariner* that his interpretation must be questioned. No critic can ever afford to disregard his own earlier experiences of a work or to despise or be ashamed of his younger self.

Coleridge is a writer about whom a great deal is known, and fresh material about him and by him is still being worked on. The other book I refer to is on a work by a writer whose life we know little about, and with whom a biographical approach is impossibly speculative and leads to circular argument. In 1953 Miss Mary Lascelles published a study of a single play by Shakespeare, *Measure for Measure*. No play has been more interpreted in the last thirty years, and in no play have critics made more persistent attempts to discover a meaning in terms of Christian thought. It has been treated almost as a Christian parable. Critics who have explored it in this way have the justification of its title, which is taken from the Gospels, of the fact that its heroine is presented to us as a novice in a religious order, and that she speaks, as few characters in Shakespeare do, a speech that is explicitly theological. At the crisis of her pleading for her brother's life, she appeals to the most central of Christian dogmas, that

> He that might the vantage best have took,
> Found out the remedy.

Miss Lascelles, whose master is Samuel Johnson, might have borrowed from him a title for her last chapter and headed it, as he headed the last chapter of *Rasselas*, 'The Conclusion, in which nothing is concluded'. She leaves her reader with no theory, no scheme of thought, but with a sense of the great tides of thought and feeling which swirl through the play and of its power to awaken in us, as the story awoke in Shakespeare, 'those ideas which slumber in the heart'. She brings to bear on the interpretation of the play knowledge of Elizabethan ways of thought, and of the Elizabethan stage and its methods of acting and producing, close study of the text and its problems, and of the difficulties of the play's language, as well as a sense of the potentialities and limitations of the artistic form in which the play is cast, tragi-comedy. The importance of Miss Lascelles's study is in the variety of approaches she makes to the central citadel of the play's significance.

She has revived, in the first place, what critics have too long pushed on one side, the study of Shakespeare's sources, what was presented to his imagination. She handles this with that sense of what is relevant to the critical problem which the new criticism has taught us. With humanity, compassion, and moral sensibility, she considers the different versions of this story which Shakespeare may have read and the various ways in which men have dealt with its cruel centre. She has found an expressive phrase for what she feels to be the story's essence in all the tellings of it. She calls it the story of 'the monstrous ransom'. The heart of this tale, to everyone who tells it, is an intolerable moral dilemma. Then, like her master Johnson, she refuses to disregard, as beneath critical notice, the judgement of what he called 'the common reader', the person whom she describes as 'the plain man trudging by'. She shirks no difficulties or anomalies; she considers patiently and sympathetically all those objections which troubled under-graduates bring to their tutors when they approach this play with their own unaided wits and natural moral sense, un-assisted by the interpreters. She ends by demonstrating, triumphantly in my view, that 'for all the perils of misunder-standing with which it is beset, the study of the characters in their relation with one another—here conditioned by the given story, there, developing free of it—remains the right approach; and its alternative, a pursuit of phantoms'. Her reward, and ours, is to be left at the end of her book not with themes and patterns but with the play. It is open to us to see what analogies we care to see. Lastly, Miss Lascelles makes no attempt to overleap the intervening centuries and somehow make herself into 'an Elizabethan'. She takes into account not merely what Shakespeare may have read, the ideas of his age, and the nuances of his language, but also how men have read him. She knows that writers cannot only be interpreted in terms of what lies behind them and around. That is to reduce genius to the level of mediocrity and forget that the reason we read Shakespeare is because he is more than 'an Elizabethan'. The disagreement over this play is a critical fact, like the extreme fluctuations of Donne's reputation. The work has come down to us through the centuries, not in a sealed box, but as something which has moved and troubled the imaginations of men. It is dangerous to disregard our own past; it is equally dangerous to disregard the past through which a work has survived. Miss Lascelles's book gathers up as it proceeds the doubts and reflections this play has provoked through the centuries which divide us from its author and its first audiences. The success of her book is that it does not arrive finally at 'the meaning of *Measure for Measure*'. She has been content to leave the play more meaningful than it was before we read her study.

This discussion is of only limited applicability to the literary criticism of the Gospels. The problems there are very different and the difficulties of interpretation far greater. I do not doubt that the 'newer method', the typological approach, throws much light on the evangelists' methods of composition and has made a significant contribution to our understanding. Speaking as a Christian, I would say that it has revealed another aspect of the *praeparatio evangelii*: the preparation of the imaginations of men to receive, when the fullness of time was come, the event of Jesus Christ and to render it to mankind. But, as a literary critic, I find it too one-sided, too abstract, intellectual and bookish, too literary and aesthetic an approach to the interpretation of the Gospels. It does not come to terms with the Gospels' proclamation of event, and their appeal through that to the moral imagination. I do not trust a literary criticism which is so unconcerned with anything but pattern and is so dominated by ideas. I realize that, however sceptical I may be about the importance of the mystical senses to men of the early seventeenth century in England, there is no question of their importance to men of late antiquity and of the early Christian centuries. All the same, the fact that many critics are capable of so over-estimating the importance of 'hidden senses' elsewhere, suggests that writers of this generation may be tempted to over-estimate the part played by this way of thinking in the production of those extraordinary literary documents, the four canonical Gospels. For if it is true that Shakespeare cannot be interpreted wholly in terms of what he shares with his contemporaries, how much more is this true of the writers of the Gospels. Their works are inexplicable in terms of contemporary Greek and Jewish literary practice.[1]

Many literary critics, like the typological critics of the New Testament, impress on their readers the necessity of trying to think in this way. Both, rather unaccountably, assume that this is very difficult for 'modern' man. They ought, possibly, to be warning us instead to be on our guard against its obvious attractiveness to many modern minds. To the aesthetic sensibility of today the symbolic presentation of Christ seems more expressive and more congenial than the attempt to picture him in his humanity. The taste of both Christian and non-Christian responds to the Christus Victor reigning robed and crowned from the Tree, to the Christ in Majesty seated amidst the Twelve, or between the Four Beasts, or to the figuring of Christ in Melchizedek, High Priest of Salem,

[1] Professor C. R. Dodd's recent study *The Interpretation of the Fourth Gospel* (1954) displays this abundantly.

standing behind his altar offering the unbloody sacrifice of bread and wine, or to his presentation as a Lamb on a green mountain from which flow the four rivers of Paradise. Such images seem to many more significant than the teaching Christ portrayed by the sculptor of *Le Beau Dieu d'Amiens*, the naked and exhausted Christ hanging from the Cross, or the Christ whom Verrocchio showed offering the wounds in his risen body to the touch of doubting Thomas. Significant art of today has closer affinities with the art of earlier Christian ages than with the art of the sculptors of the thirteenth and fourteenth centuries in France or than with the art of the high Renaissance. The creative artist may value or neglect the art of past ages according as it is, or is not, related to his own art, just as the philosopher will think important those philosophers who were concerned with problems similar to those with which he is himself concerned. But the critic or scholar has a different function from that of the artist or original thinker. One of his uses is to help to preserve the creative thought of his own day from provincialism in time, by keeping alive and available to his own age what is neglected or disparaged by those absorbed in the preoccupations of the hour. His humble task is to protect his betters from the corruption of fashions.

Many readers of the Gospels today and many writers on them seem to see a very different figure from the Christ who fed with publicans and sinners and set a little child in the midst. This was possibly the dominant literary image of Christ in the nineteenth century. The dominant literary image today is more often of a lonely figure walking ahead of his puzzled and half-frightened disciples, speaking to them abruptly in dark riddles, with his face set to go up to Jerusalem.

The texts quoted as expressive of the Christ who walked on this earth are not texts such as 'Suffer the little children to come unto me', but rather texts such as 'I have a baptism to be baptized with; and how am I straitened till it be accomplished'. The theologian of today may rightly concentrate on whatever image best illuminates his present concern; but the literary critic cannot disregard the other images. Much of the literary criticism of the Gospels in the nineteenth century may be justly charged with sentimentality. Its authors might well retort upon some of their successors the countercharge of inhumanity. It is a charge which can be brought against much of the art and literature of this age.

PRINTED IN GREAT BRITAIN
AT THE UNIVERSITY PRESS, OXFORD
BY VIVIAN RIDLER
PRINTER TO THE UNIVERSITY

Date Due